In *Radical like Jesus*, my friend Greg is inviting you i̶ will transform you into a flourishing follower of Jesus .... guide, Greg will take you by the hand and show you how to become radical like Jesus! Get this book and read it with five of your friends. Grow together!

    DERWIN GRAY, cofounder and lead pastor of Transformation Church, author of *Lit Up with Love*

Greg Stier has written a Christ-centered, biblically grounded, and from-the-heart guide to what a normal Christian life should be, but for most of us, it is a radical one. *Radical like Jesus* is a clear and engaging call to follow him and share his good news with others. I highly recommend it.

    RANDY ALCORN, author of *Heaven*, *Happiness*, and *Giving Is the Good Life*

Courageous and compelling, personal and practical, this book by my friend Greg Stier will encourage you, inspire you, and motivate you to emulate the boldness of Jesus in your everyday life. It's all the more powerful because I've seen how Greg already models these qualities himself. Don't peruse this book—absorb it and put its thoroughly biblical principles into daily action. I'm thankful I've been able to watch as Greg has faithfully embodied the grace and truth of Jesus, and I'm thrilled to learn from his experiences how to live an ever-more radical life for the sake of the gospel.

    LEE STROBEL, *New York Times* bestselling writer, author of *The Case for Christ* and *Is God Real?*

Greg's work is an inviting, challenging exploration of radical life in and with Jesus Christ, by one who practices and shares it with millions of young believers. I highly recommend this book for any young person, especially one with a heart to be intimate with Christ and serve him radically. . . . This is a book I would buy and present to any young person who desires to fully live the "radical life for Christ," following in Jesus' obedient footsteps to the cross and resurrection as Greg emulates in his calling.

    TOM PHILLIPS, senior advisor for the Billy Graham Evangelistic Association

I've been leading in some capacity for over forty years, the last thirty at Dare 2 Share alongside Greg Stier. Greg has a way of breaking down challenging biblical truths in a way that makes them easy to understand and apply. His recent book, *Radical like Jesus*, is his best yet. After reading it, I'm challenged but not overwhelmed. Any Christ follower can be radical like Jesus!

    DEBBIE BRESINA, president of Dare 2 Share

At a time when our culture has become conditioned to prioritize comfort, prosperity, and human accolades, Greg Stier reminds us that we're called to become more and more like Jesus—and that looks very different from the world's idea of success. During his earthly ministry, Jesus was a radical follower of his Father in heaven, and we have the privilege of walking in his footsteps. In his latest book, Greg will help point you to the kind of disciplines and lifestyle that reflect a radical, world-changing submission to Christ.

JIM DALY, president of Focus on the Family

Back in 2015, Greg and I had the privilege of taking a deep dive into Jesus together, walking where Jesus walked in the land of Israel. I've known Greg for many years, and his zeal for the gospel is unquestioned and unmatched. But in Israel, I saw a different zeal, one revealed in the pages of *Radical like Jesus*. The apostle Paul's words in Philippians 3:10 reflect the passion deeply rooted in Greg's soul: "I want to know Christ!" Page after page of *Radical like Jesus* will reveal that passion and fuel that same passion deep in your soul. As I've heard my friend say many times, "Fall in love with evangelism, and you will fizzle out. But fall in love with Jesus, and you will share him forever!" *Radical like Jesus* will fan the flames of your first love for Jesus, and you won't be able to contain your desire to share him with others.

DOUG HOLLIDAY, president of Sonlife

I can't imagine a more important message for the contemporary church to hear: we are not just called to make converts to Jesus, but disciples of Jesus. In his book *Radical like Jesus*, Greg Stier reminds us that Christianity is a radical call to imitate the radical way of Jesus with everything we have. I am praying that this book gets a wide reading as we learn to become more committed followers of Jesus.

DR. JT ENGLISH, pastor, professor, and author

A lot of people talk about wanting to be "sold out," "all-in," or "radical" . . . and then there are a few that live it out in real life. My friend Greg Stier is one of those people. His radical passion for Jesus and the message of the gospel is both genuine and inspiring. His latest book gives us a powerful, practical game plan directly from the Scriptures to be radical like Jesus every day.

KRISTOPHER STOUT, executive vice president of international ministries, Word of Life Fellowship

God is calling you to be a part of something big? What is that, and how do you find it? In *Radical like Jesus*, Greg Stier walks us through the radical life Jesus is calling us to and gives us practical steps for beginning that journey. I dare you to pick up this book and start practicing it. If you do, your life will never be the same.

SEAN McDOWELL, PhD, professor of apologetics at Biola University, popular YouTuber, and author of *A Rebel's Manifesto*

This incredible project is much more than a book. Greg has drawn a map to experiencing and sharing an abundant, gospel-advancing life and knowing God as our always-by-our-side, radical guide.

KATHY BRANZELL, president of National Day of Prayer Task Force

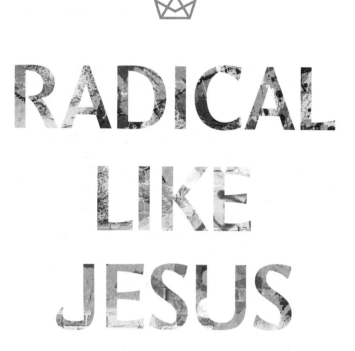

RADICAL LIKE JESUS

21 Challenges to Live a Revolutionary Life

GREG STIER

TYNDALE
MOMENTUM®

A Tyndale nonfiction imprint

For information about special discounts for bulk purchases, please contact Tyndale House Publishers at csresponse@tyndale.com, or call 1-855-277-9400.

Library of Congress Cataloging-in-Publication Data

A catalog record for this book is available from the Library of Congress.

ISBN 978-1-4964-8465-9

Printed in the United States of America

30	29	28	27	26	25	24
7	6	5	4	3	2	1

Foreword

When I first met Greg Stier during Winter Jam, I was captured by his ability to communicate the saving power of Jesus with clarity and conviction. When you're preaching to a packed-out room of thousands of teens and young adults, this is no small feat. In just fifteen minutes, Greg managed to share how God had completely transformed his life and walked every person in that arena through the entirety of the gospel.

Greg has a passion for evangelism that is unlike many people I've met and a vision to see a generation rise up to live on mission for Jesus. The biggest hurdle to this generation coming to know Jesus is simply whether or not people who know the truth are willing to step out and share it. Greg has blazed a trail around the world to equip and implore teens and young adults to make much of Jesus and his Kingdom.

The more you get to know Greg, the more you see how he lives every day radically on mission like Jesus modeled for us in his time on planet Earth. Greg desires to serve the Lord by being intellectually, physically, relationally, and spiritually strong in order to share the Good News of Jesus—wherever, however, and whenever. Through the pages of *Radical like Jesus*, Greg invites us to walk in these rhythms and take action toward twenty-one specific challenges so that Jesus will live through us and that we might do the things he did.

Greg is a testament to the transformation that comes from a lifetime of following Jesus. He masterfully teaches through the Scriptures while introducing and explaining essential theological anchors for the Christian life. He weaves together profound biblical stories, powerful personal anecdotes, and relatable parallels to create a tapestry that connects ancient biblical truths with our lives today.

This book isn't a self-help resource—it's the very heart of the gospel. Never losing sight of Jesus, Greg constantly sets his gaze on the King—the only one who saves. Greg writes, "Ultimately, Jesus didn't come to this earth to show us how to live a radical life. He came to give us life—new life, true life, eternal life that starts now and lasts forever."

This message is crucial. *Radical like Jesus* is a timely reminder of the relentless pursuit of Jesus' love and the importance of carrying the gospel to the ends of the Earth. I pray this resource makes you hungrier for the things of God and more dependent on Jesus than ever before. As you are transformed in the way of Jesus, empowered to share the gospel that all may know his name, and stretched beyond your daily routines, I pray that God meets you just where you are and continues to pour out his love and mercy over your life.

May we all take up the mantle of Greg's challenge to live radically, like Jesus did.

Louie Giglio
Pastor of Passion City Church, founder of Passion Conferences

Introduction

One of those days Jesus went out to a mountainside to pray,
and spent the night praying to God.

LUKE 6:12

As I type these words, I'm sitting alone in the mountains of Colorado in the pitch-black darkness of night. The only light for miles around is from my laptop. It's 3:23 a.m. I haven't seen one person since I arrived yesterday.

I'm perched on a large boulder above Moraine Park, located in the Rocky Mountain National Park. Armed with nothing but a flashlight, bug spray, and bear spray (and my laptop), I'm doing something, well, radical like Jesus.

A few months ago, my Bible reading took me to Luke 6:12: "One of those days Jesus went out to a mountainside to pray, and spent the night praying to God." I had scheduled the last of my *Radical like Jesus* writing retreats for nearby Estes Park, Colorado. So I thought, *I've been camping before, but never by myself. And I've never spent the whole night praying to God in the mountains. That's what I'll do. I'll celebrate finishing the book by doing something radical like Jesus.*

So late yesterday afternoon I hiked into the backcountry of this vast, spectacular national park and spent the night praying on a mountainside . . . just like Jesus.

It wasn't as easy as I'd expected. For one thing, there was no moon. It got really dark, really quickly. Also, just as a sidenote, when you scan your flashlight across a large meadow at night and see two shining objects side by side, you're being watched. The meadow grass was two feet tall, and the eyes watching me hovered just above the twenty-four-inch mark. That was unsettling. Was it a coyote? A mountain lion? A bear?

Another thing I didn't plan on was how hard it was to stay awake all night. More than fear of a bear, my hardest battle was the cage match with the sleep monster. A few times throughout the night I felt typical like Peter instead of radical like Jesus. I kept nodding off over my folded hands instead of keeping watch in prayer.

But despite my battle with heavy eyelids, I had some amazing times of prayer and worship throughout the long, dark night. My main prayer was that I would be radical like Jesus and that, after reading this book, you will be too.

What does it actually mean to be radical like Jesus? Well, allow me to make the case that nobody who ever lived was as radical as Jesus. He spoke the unspeakable, declaring the truth in the midst of a culture of lies. He did the unthinkable, cleansing the Temple of hundreds (if not thousands) of money changers who were using the sacrificial system to enrich themselves. He accomplished the unbelievable, healing countless people of horrible diseases and maladies. He reached the unreachable, pouring his life into the bad, the broken, and the bullied (and even the bullies) to rescue them from the hell they were going through and headed to.

To be radical like Jesus means to speak the unspeakable, do the unthinkable, accomplish the unbelievable, and reach the unreachable . . . just like Jesus did.

You may be thinking, *There's no way. Jesus is the Son of God. I could never be like him.* But you're wrong. Consider this bold statement in 1 John 2:6: "Whoever claims to live in him must live as Jesus did."

If you are in Christ, you can live like Jesus did.

You and I can be radical like Jesus. In fact, as the verse puts it, we *must* live like Jesus did.

How is this possible? Because of the theological reality found in Galatians 2. Here Paul gives us the secret to his spiritual success. If there was anyone in the history of the church who was radical like Jesus, it was the apostle Paul. Through the power of Christ in him, he took the gospel from Jerusalem to Rome and everywhere in between across multiple mission trips. And in this single verse, he tells us his secret:

> I have been crucified with Christ and I no longer live,
> but Christ lives in me. The life I now live in the body,
> I live by faith in the Son of God, who loved me and
> gave himself for me.
>
> GALATIANS 2:20

You can be radical like Jesus because, if you are a believer in Jesus, he lives in you and wants to live through you.

What does this look like? It looks like you doing radical things in his power and for his glory. You can touch those no one else dares touch. You can heal those who seem beyond help. You can extend God's grace to the worst of the worst and challenge those who think they are the best of the best. It also means you may wash dirty feet from time to time and get crucified—verbally, anyway.

But before you can be radical like Jesus, you need to be radically transformed by Jesus.

Ultimately, Jesus didn't come to this earth to show us how to live a radical life. He came to give us life—new life, true life, eternal life that starts now and lasts forever.

Maybe you are reading this book and you are not sure you have received this gift of eternal life from Jesus. Maybe you *hope* you have it, but don't *know* for sure. Allow me to explain how you can know you have eternal life.

God loves you so much, and he created you to be in a relationship with him. The problem is sin. Our sin separates us from God. Although God loves us, he hates our sin because it violates his holy character and keeps us away from him.

You may be thinking, *I live a pretty good life. I think I'm good with the big man upstairs.* No offense, but no you don't, no you're not, and he's not "the big man upstairs." He is the unfathomably righteous God of the universe who one day will judge the living and the dead, including you and me.

His standard is perfection, nothing less. You must be as good as he is to be in his perfect presence. Trying to live up to his standard of perfection is like trying to hurdle Mount Everest.

In short, we are sinners condemned to hell, and there's nothing we can do about it in ourselves.

So God did something about it.

Two thousand years ago God sent his only Son into the world to live the perfect life we could never live and to die in our place because of our sin. Three days later he rose from the dead, proving he was God in the flesh. Now, everyone who simply believes that Jesus died in their place for their sin and trusts in Jesus alone to save them from their sins, has eternal life. And this new life with Jesus starts now and lasts forever.

The most famous verse of the Bible puts it this way: "God so loved the world that he gave his one and only Son, that whoever believes in him shall not perish but have eternal life" (John 3:16).

If you've never put your faith in Jesus and received that free gift of eternal life, do it right now. Receive the free gift of eternal life by faith in Jesus based on his finished work on the cross. This means that you are fully trusting in Jesus as your only way of going to heaven. Not Jesus *and* doing good, going to church, being religious, or anything else, just Jesus alone. As soon as you do, the Holy Spirit will come to live inside you and give you the ability to be radical like Jesus in every way, because Jesus himself will be living through you!

If you have already put your faith in Jesus (or did just now), you are ready to tackle the challenge of being radical like Jesus. You are ready to take following him to the next level.

At the end of every chapter in this book, you will find a Radical like Jesus Challenge. When we live in the power of the Spirit and allow God to do radical things through us, you and I can change our world!

This book is about doing, not just learning. Yes, I pray you get some game-changing insights into Jesus while you read it. But putting what you learn into practice is really what following Jesus is all about.

Some challenges will be easy. Others will be hard. A few will be somewhere in between. Do not skip the challenges. The book is built around them. If you're not ready to be a doer of the word and want to be a hearer only (see James 1:22), I encourage you to return this book and get your money back.

But I'm praying there's a doer inside you who is hungry for a challenge and thirsty for a risk. I'm hoping that deep down you are tired of reading about revivals—you want to experience one. I'm optimistic that you are not satisfied with hearing stories about others doing great things for God—you want to do some yourself.

That's why this book is great for studying and applying as a couple or a small group. You can hold each other accountable to do the Radical like Jesus Challenges chapter after chapter and share the stories of what God did as a result.

As I finish writing these words perched atop my big rock,

the sun's predawn illumination has turned the pitch black into a beautiful morning glow. Soon it will breach the mountain-shaped horizon.

I pray the truths of this book will break upon the horizon of your heart and that, as a result of putting these truths into practice, the Son will shine on you and through you like never before.

I pray both of us will become radical like Jesus.

1

BE

*"But why did you need to search?" he asked. "Didn't you know that I must
be in my Father's house?" But they didn't understand what he meant.*

LUKE 2:49-50, NLT

I WAS A TERRIFIED KID. Being raised in the highest crime rate area
of my city, I was afraid of the rampant gangs and street violence
that swarmed my house like mosquitos on un-DEETed skin in a
hot jungle mess. And the danger wasn't just outside my house. It
was inside too.

My family was known as "that family," the one you wanted to
avoid in a street fight, the one that would call all muscular hands
on deck to punch the opposition in the teeth.

When someone yelled "fight," everyone would pile out of our
house like a commando squad eager to beat whoever we were fighting to a pulp. Everyone except me.

I was a quiet, scared, and scarred fatherless kid who was afraid
of my own skinny-boy shadow. My bodybuilding, street-fighting,

fist-throwing, headbutting uncles, aunts, and cousins were the epitome of tough. I was the epitome of not-enough-of-the-tough-stuff.

My solace was not in cracking skulls but in cracking books, specifically the Bible. The little red King James Version that Mrs. Muirhead, my second-grade Sunday school teacher, gave me was the book I cherished most. It was the Bible I took with me when I holed up underneath the kitchen sink to get away from all the sirens, screams, and sounds of fists hitting flesh-padded jawbones.

Nestled between the protruding pipes and cleaning supplies, my small body contorted until it was comfortable. In one hand was my little red Bible; in my other hand was a flashlight.

For years I had been going underneath that kitchen sink seeking solace and silence. At eight years old, it was a time of scouring Scripture. The *thees* and *thous* of the Shakespearean-era Bible translation began to make sense to my overactive mind as the closed cabinet doors muffled the yells of a loud and violent family. That two-foot-by-three-foot space became my quiet place, my sacred space, my place to just *be* with my newfound heavenly Father.

BEING WITH THE HEAVENLY FATHER

To become radical like Jesus we must be intentional, passionate, and curious when it comes to spending time with the Father.

Nobody embodied this more than young Jesus. Although there is but one New Testament passage about him during his preteen and early teen years (see Luke 2:40-52), these thirteen verses are packed with insights about the boy-about-to-become-a-man and his singular passion to be with the Father.

In Jewish culture, the transition from boyhood to manhood took place at the age of thirteen. In this passage of Scripture, Jesus was twelve and on the brink of manhood. At the end of his family's annual trip to Jerusalem for the Passover celebration, he was left behind and found himself in the Temple courts for three days, asking questions of the rabbis and giving profound answers to their questions. By the time Mary and Joseph found him, there was a crowd of teachers surrounding him who were astounded by the gravitas of his answers and the penetrating profundity of his questions.

When Mary rebuked Jesus for his decision to stay in Jerusalem instead of traveling with the caravan back to Nazareth, he simply answered, "Didn't you know that I must be in my Father's house?" (verse 49, NLT).

It is clear from this passage that Jesus was fully aware of who his real Father was—not Joseph, but Yahweh. It is also clear that Jesus longed to be with his Father in his house, the Temple.

The Temple was considered God's house, his dwelling place among the Israelites (see Exodus 25:8-9). Why? It was no longer because the presence of God dwelled in the Holy of Holies. Ezekiel 10 describes the horrific scene of God's glory leaving the Temple once and for all. The presence of God that hovered behind the veil of the Holy of Holies returned to heaven.

But now the glory of God had returned to the Temple in the skin of a twelve-year-old named Jesus. This young man was the glorious presence of God that had returned to the God-forsaken Temple of the Jews.

Why did Jesus enjoy being in his Father's house? Although a direct answer is not given in this verse, the underlying answer is hidden beneath the surface, waiting to be dug up.

Jesus longed to be where God's Word was being publicly read and explained.

Jesus didn't emerge from Mary's womb quoting the Torah. No, he had to learn to read, go to synagogue school like every other

Jewish boy, memorize Scripture, and assimilate it. Most scholars assume that this was all part of his growing-up years in Nazareth. And because asking questions of a rabbi was core to the learning style of the Jews, it's highly likely that Jesus had exhausted the local Galilean rabbis with his in-depth, penetrating questions.

But now he was in the big leagues. These were experts in the law and the prophets. He was speaking to the top Torah teachers of his time—the Chuck Swindolls, the Erwin Lutzers, the Tony Evanses of the time.

Jesus was asking questions, processing their answers, honing his theology, and arriving at biblical conclusions. He was doing this before the best of the best—and they were shocked at his depth of understanding. The word used here for "understanding" in the original Greek is *sunesis*, which means "a bringing together." The implication is that Jesus was utilizing synthesized reasoning to connect the dots in ways that bring deeper insights than the rabbinical teachers had previously considered.

This was Jesus' version of being underneath a kitchen sink with a flashlight and a Bible. He was searching for spiritual truth. But unlike me, he found these truths much more quickly, uninhibited by sin or a clouded relationship with God.

If we want to learn to be like Jesus when it comes to being with our heavenly Father, there are three stark principles for us from this story: Be intentional. Be curious. Be passionate.

BE INTENTIONAL

Luke 2:41-42 says, "Every year Jesus' parents went to Jerusalem for the Passover festival. When Jesus was twelve years old, they attended the festival *as usual*" (emphasis added, NLT). The annual festivals were attended "as usual" by every committed Jew. In the Jewish culture, males were commanded to attend three festivals in person per year: Passover (also known as the Feast of Unleavened Bread), the Feast of Weeks (Pentecost), and the Feast of Tabernacles (see Exodus 23:14-19).

Yet Jesus had more than just three annual festival "as usuals" in his life. He most likely had personal times of learning from his earthly father, daily times of Torah mastery, weekly times of learning at the synagogue as a family, and, of course, his own time of meditation on God's Word.

The Holy Scriptures were central to his "as usuals." They were central to his time at the Temple and synagogue. They were central to his home life and personal life.

Are they central to yours?

We are living in a culture of Christianity where five-minute app devotionals (which are better than not having devotionals at all!) have replaced deep, reflective, and prayerful reading, study, and meditation on God's Word.

Most Christians I know have never read the Bible cover to cover. They skim the top of texts like rocks skipping on water. But God desires us to plunge deeply into his Word, like a large anchor plummets to the depths of the ocean. Listen to the words of David:

> The law of the LORD is perfect,
>   refreshing the soul.
> The statutes of the LORD are trustworthy,
>   making wise the simple.
> The precepts of the LORD are right,
>   giving joy to the heart.
> The commands of the LORD are radiant,
>   giving light to the eyes.
> The fear of the LORD is pure,
>   enduring forever.

The decrees of the LORD are firm,
  and all of them are righteous.

They are more precious than gold,
  than much pure gold;
they are sweeter than honey,
  than honey from the honeycomb.
By them your servant is warned;
  in keeping them there is great reward.

PSALM 19:7-11

God's Word is perfect, refreshing, trustworthy, right, radiant, pure, firm, righteous, precious, and sweet. David believed this. Jesus, the Son of David, believed this. They scoured the Scriptures because they believed this.

Do *you* believe this? Do your "as usuals" reflect this?

- Your annual "as usuals" of spiritual retreats, Bible conferences, etc.
- Your weekly "as usuals" of church attendance, Bible study, small group, etc.
- Your daily "as usuals" of time reading and reflecting on God's Word, journaling, etc.

In his book *Atomic Habits*, James Clear writes, "Every action you take is a vote for the type of person you wish to become."[1] If we want to be like Jesus, then we must have habits like Jesus.

Jesus mastered Scripture. He read it, meditated on it, memorized it, and obeyed it. So should we.

The Bible is worthy of our highest attention and deepest devotion. God's Word is inspired (see 2 Timothy 3:16-17), therefore inerrant (see Proverbs 30:5), therefore in charge (see James 1:22).

It is the true north of our compass that will keep us from getting lost. It is our strong anchor in a stormy sea that will keep us from drifting from God. It is our soft couch upon which we rest when we are exhausted. It is the tent we set up so we can be alone with God.

Be intentional like Jesus. Make spending time with God in his Word your biggest "as usual."

BE CURIOUS

I was a troublesome student. I terrorized my teachers—not because I was not paying attention or because I was goofing around all the time (although I did a lot of that). No, I terrorized my teachers because if I didn't understand a subject or a concept, I would relentlessly ask questions until they explained it well enough for me to understand. I'm a slow learner, but a determined one.

Jesus was a *fast* and determined learner. He was curious. His sharp mind, uninhibited by sin and distraction, worked so quickly that it astounded the top teachers of his time. Luke describes it this way: "Three days later they finally discovered him in the Temple, sitting among the religious teachers, listening to them and asking questions. All who heard him were amazed at his understanding and his answers" (2:46-47, NLT).

Jesus asked questions and assimilated answers. He wrestled through subjects until he wrestled them fully to the ground and pinned them down.

We should have such an approach when we take time to be with our Father. Ask God hard questions, and wrestle through difficult subjects. Do the same with the preachers and teachers in your world. Be curious, and don't stop asking hard questions until you get the answers from God's Word—even if you're a slow learner like me.

BE PASSIONATE

Jesus was so passionate about being in his Father's house and understanding his Father's Word that he spent three days and nights in the Temple, without his family, as a twelve-year-old boy.

Where did Jesus sleep during these three days? How did he eat? *Did* he eat? Did he care?

It seems like the only thing on his mind was understanding God's Word better. During these seventy-two hours, he relentlessly quizzed the rabbis. He was passionate to understand as much as he possibly could before his parents found him.

It wasn't just the acquisition of knowledge. He didn't want just to know more; he wanted to grow more, to love his Father with perfect love and obey him with perfect submission. That was his passion. That was his obsession. That's what made food, sleep, rest, and the safety of being with Mom and Dad a distant second.

Jesus was passionate about being with the Father and knowing his Word.

I'm a passionate guy. When I preach, the veins in my neck pop and I sweat like Tommy Boy in a sauna with a broken thermostat. As someone once said, "When I preach, I set myself on fire and people come to watch me burn."

But as passionate as I am about preaching, I want to be more passionate about my time with God in his Word.

For years I traveled with the spoken word artist Jason Petty (aka Propaganda). Jason, Zane Black, and I traveled the nation training teens how to share the gospel during our Dare 2 Share conferences. Jason used to say to the teenagers, "When it comes to your time with the Lord, be a jerk about it."

We need to pick a time and place we meet with God every single day. That place becomes our version of our "Father's house."

My "Father's house" is at the end of our long couch by the

gas fireplace. Every morning, "as usual," I meet him there. I seek to spend the first hour of every day with God. During this time, I pray, read his Word, meditate on it, and sometimes journal a prayer back to God about a verse that really communicates to me. I ask God the hard questions. I wrestle through difficult passages until the Holy Spirit, the ultimate teacher, helps me understand. And then I seek to put whatever truth I've learned that day into practice in some tangible way.

People often ask me if I ever went through a time of rebellion against God. I haven't. To be sure, I have struggled with sin and faltered and failed, but I have never stopped fighting the good fight to be holy and to serve Christ.

When they ask how I can explain this, the only answer I can give them is that I am relentlessly in God's Word every single day, seeking his will, asking him to fill me with his power to conquer the temptations of that day.

I have chosen to be in my Father's house. And by God's grace, I will never leave.

Join me there.

RADICAL LIKE JESUS CHALLENGE #1
Difficulty: Easy

Set a daily time and place to meet with the Lord for at least fifteen minutes.

Make it your goal to do this for at least twenty-one days in a row to create an unshakable and unbreakable habit.

2

GROW

*Jesus grew in wisdom and in stature and in favor
with God and all the people.*

LUKE 2:52, NLT

WHEN I GRADUATED FROM HIGH SCHOOL, I had 8 percent body fat. This made even tiny muscles like mine look defined and impressive.

But between the ages of twenty-five and twenty-eight, I got extremely out of shape. My added poundage was not from lifting weights but from curling forks. I had eaten my way from 155 pounds as a senior in high school to 223 pounds as a young pastor in Denver. Walking up the stairs felt like climbing Mount Everest. I was so out of shape that I got super tired throughout the day. Soon I started taking naps mid-afternoon just to get my energy back. My doctors were starting to get concerned about high blood pressure, too much cholesterol, and the possibility of heart disease.

How did I end up like this?

Believe it or not, I blame Michael Jackson.

Although I was raised in an independent fundamentalist church, I was always a closet dancer—actually, a basement dancer. I used the full length of my grandparents' basement, which I lived in during my high school years, as my own personal dance studio.

I would watch shows like *American Bandstand* and *Soul Train* to learn how to dance. Then I'd dance for hours in that basement to the latest disco, pop, or whatever.

Thank the Lord, none of my tough, street-fighting family ever found out about my secret dancing life. It's hard to dance with broken knees.

Over the years I became quite the dancer. By my junior year of college at Colorado Christian University, I was a dancing fool. My buddies and I won a talent show called "O'Malley's Alley" by doing our own version of Michael Jackson's "Bad" video. From coordinated fight scenes to backflips to crisp, pre-orchestrated moves, we stunned the crowd and won the prize.

Flash forward four years, and I was a twenty-five-year-old, newly married pastor—dressed up in my suit about to do some hospital visitation—when something happened that changed everything. The Michael Jackson "Bad" video came on television. I couldn't help myself. I started dancing to impress my wife, did the splits, just like I had done four years earlier. I spun my whole body around in a way that would make MJ proud . . . except this time, my foot got caught in our shag carpet. My right foot stayed facing forward while my whole body spun 360 degrees. Snap, boom, scream—I fell to the ground. I tore my ACL, the major ligament that runs directly through the knee.

After major knee surgery, I got lazy and failed to complete my rehab. I only did three out of the eight weeks of stretching and strength training recommended.

I developed a pronounced limp. No more dancing. No more basketball. No more exercise. But lots more food.

When my knee hurt, I ate.

When someone said, "Let's go to the gym," I went to the fridge.

When I got depressed about gaining weight, I'd have another bowl of ice cream.

I was a rapidly growing pastor of a rapidly growing church who vastly underestimated the impact being out of shape was having on all areas of my life. I was short-tempered with my wife and less committed to my time with God. I didn't have the energy to hang with my friends. Every night when I came home, I would just sit in front of the television and fall asleep, exhausted. Something had to change.

Thank God for a bodybuilding friend of mine, Donnie Coxsey. One day after a guest preacher used my body as an example of people being spiritually out of shape, Donnie pulled me aside and said, "Enough is enough. I'm taking you to the gym."

Donnie put me on a workout regimen and gave me a nutrition plan that helped me get back into shape.

By the time I was thirty, I was 185 pounds and much healthier. By God's grace, I've been able to remain in decent shape since then.

Putting God at the center of how you view health and fitness can change you. Your body is "the temple of the Holy Spirit" (1 Corinthians 6:19, NLT), so some sort of "temple maintenance" is appropriate. Then you can serve him with the energy and endurance he deserves.

But it is not just in the physical arena that we need to honor God. We can honor him on every level of our personal growth, just like Jesus did.

Luke 2:52 tells us, "Jesus grew in wisdom and in stature and in favor with God and all the people" (NLT).

Jesus grew in four areas: wisdom, stature, favor with God, and favor with people. Another way to say this is that he grew intellectually, physically, spiritually, and relationally. From the time he was young, Jesus focused on putting God right in the center of his personal growth.

When the text says that Jesus "grew" in these areas, it uses the Greek verb *prokopto*, which means growth by conscious and consistent effort. To lead a radical life, we, too, must make a conscious and consistent effort to grow in these four areas.

INTELLECTUAL GROWTH

Jesus grew intellectually. How? The simple answer is through the synagogue school that every Jewish boy attended during their growing-up years. The education of young Jewish children was intense. Authors Roy B. Blizzard and David Bivin, citing extra-biblical written sources, describe Jesus' early childhood and adolescence as being filled with studying and memorizing vast quantities of Scripture, as well as commentaries and rabbinic legal rulings. This was the standard scholastic training for Jewish boys. According to Blizzard and Bivin, "It is important to emphasize that this was exactly what most of the other children of His day were doing. To such an extent that most of the people in Jesus' day had large portions of this literature firmly committed to memory, and at the very least, almost all the *Old Testament*."[1]

We must grow intellectually, just like Jesus. This means we must be well-read, just like Jesus. We must think deeply, just like Jesus. We must be conversant on different subjects and have a voracious appetite to learn more. Of course, we must see everything through the lens of Scripture. But as followers of Jesus, we must grow in both knowledge and wisdom, which is the proper use of that knowledge.

In his classic book, Mark Noll writes, "The scandal of the evangelical mind is that there is not much of an evangelical mind."[2]

May we as Christians have a thirst to learn. As Saint Augustine taught, all truth is God's truth.[3]

The more we know, the more wisdom we can have, the better decisions we can make, the more we can converse with others intelligently and use those conversations to point more people to Jesus.

PHYSICAL GROWTH

Jesus grew strong physically.

Think about his diet. He ate fish, lamb, fruit, vegetables, and bread—all prepared without preservatives or chemicals.

Jesus walked everywhere. Some have estimated that during his earthly ministry, Jesus walked 3,125 miles.[4]

Jesus was a carpenter, which means he had a manual labor job that was physically demanding. Jesus was most likely ripped. He ate well, walked far, and lifted heavy things. Consider how much Jesus went through physically when he was tortured and crucified. He had to have been in extremely good shape to endure being beaten "beyond human likeness" (Isaiah 52:14) and mercilessly whipped by Roman soldiers. A lesser man physically may not have made it through the beating to the cross.

Scripture doesn't tell us at what age Jesus became self-aware of his role as Savior of the world, but I believe he had his eyes on the cross long before he entered into his public ministry at age thirty. He would need to be strong enough physically to endure what awaited him when he paid the price for the sin of humanity with his own innocent life.

What an example for us.

Are you taking care of yourself physically? Do you sleep enough? Are you eating healthy? Do you exercise?

Getting and staying in shape will give you the energy and endurance for the mission God has given you in life. It will help you bear the cross God has called you to carry. Refuse to make health and fitness a god, but use your body to serve God.

SPIRITUAL GROWTH

Jesus grew "in favor with God." It's sometimes hard to reconcile this phrase with the reality that Jesus was the Son of God. But Jesus was fully God and fully human. And he lived his life as a human fully dependent on God.

As a human Jesus set the pace for spiritual growth. He had a plan to grow to know his Father, love his Father, and serve his Father.

Part of this had to be sharpening and perfecting his personal spiritual disciplines. The Christian ministry Cru refers to ten spiritual disciplines we can exercise as believers: Bible reading, Bible study, Bible memorization, prayer, generosity, fellowship, fasting, silence, simplicity, and celebration.[5] While different Christian leaders and organizations have different lists for what are considered spiritual disciplines, this is a solid compilation.

As I read through this list, I can imagine Jesus applying all these spiritual disciplines while he was growing up.

The discipline of prayer was a huge focus for him. We see him throughout the Gospels escaping ministry opportunities to go off by himself to pray. His prayer life must have been honed as a young man in Nazareth. I imagine he frequently climbed the hills that surrounded his small country village and found caves and overlooks where he could pour out his heart to his Father in prayer.

When Jesus' earthly ministry officially kicked off with forty days in the wilderness, it began with forty days of fasting. It's impossible for me to fathom that this was the first time Jesus fasted for an extended amount of time. Perhaps this was his longest fast, but if I were a betting man (which is *not* a spiritual discipline), I'd push all my money to the middle of the table to wager that Jesus had been fasting as a spiritual discipline since he was a young man.

And much of Jesus' earthly ministry was silence and simplicity. He lived homeless during these years, didn't carry many (if any) worldly possessions with him, and often got away for times of silence so that he could pray.

All the spiritual disciplines reflected in the earthly ministry of Jesus had very likely been part of his spiritual growth since he was a young man.

RELATIONAL GROWTH

Jesus grew in favor with people.

If you think about Jesus as a son, a brother (he was the oldest of several siblings according to Matthew 13:55-56), a friend, a coworker, and a neighbor, it gives you a different perspective on him.

Jesus grew relationally as a son. After he stayed behind at the Temple in Jerusalem for three days and was rebuked by his mother for it, "he returned to Nazareth with them and was obedient to them" (Luke 2:51, NLT).

How was Jesus as a big brother? I'm sure his siblings couldn't help feeling somewhat intimidated by him because he never complained (see 1 Peter 2:23) or sinned (see 2 Corinthians 5:21). He did all things well. When a sibling does all things well, it can lead to jealousy and comparison. But regardless of how his brothers and sisters felt about him, he loved them with perfect love. Yes, he did all things well, including being a big brother.

Jesus grew relationally on every level. He became a better son, brother, friend, coworker, and neighbor. He consciously and consistently grew in his relationship with others. I'm sure no mother had a son who ever obeyed more, no sibling had a brother who ever listened better, and no friend had a friend who ever cared more.

GOD IN THE QUAD

Scripture indicates that Jesus grew intellectually, physically, spiritually, and relationally, and just as he grew in these four areas for the glory of God, so can we.

But how?

I call it putting "God in the Quad." Over the last several years, I've focused on these four areas of growth in my life (the Quad). I have a list of specific goals in each area. These goals are measurable and specific. Like Jesus, I want to grow in the Quad consciously and consistently.

To give you a sample of my "God in the Quad" goals, here is one specific goal in each of the four areas:

Intellectual	Physical
Listen to podcasts that will stretch my mind and make me think every week.	Work out for 45 minutes every day (weights or spin cycle).
Spiritual	**Relational**
Spend the first hour of every day in God's Word and prayer.	Have a date with my wife every week.

"Jesus grew in wisdom and stature and in favor with God and all the people." So must we.

Fill out the "God in the Quad" form below, putting one specific, measurable goal in each quadrant. Choose one area to focus on (intellectual, physical, spiritual, or relational) until it becomes a habit, then keep adding until each becomes a regular rhythm.

Intellectual		**Physical**
Spiritual		**Relational**

BUILD

"Isn't this the carpenter? Isn't this Mary's son and the brother
of James, Joseph, Judas and Simon? Aren't his sisters here with us?"
And they took offense at him.

MARK 6:3

IT WAS A SCORCHING HOT SUMMER DAY, and I was still on the roof.

For the last four summers I had taken up roofing to pay the bills. Although I had just graduated from high school, I needed money for my car, gas, insurance, and, of course, college, which was coming up in late August. I had to make money doing the only thing I really knew how to do—roof.

One of my youth leaders, Kenny Sanchez, had a roofing company with his big brother, Greg. These two solid believers were committed to high-quality roofing, and I was glad to have the job. But roofing was hard, and some of it got technical.

While I was pretty good at being the "gopher" (bucking shingles up ladders and moving heavy stuff from here to there), I wasn't the best roofer on a technical level. I tried my hardest, but I knew this wasn't my calling. From the time I preached my first real sermon at my grandfather's funeral when I was fifteen years old, I knew I was called to be a preacher, an evangelist.

So I was super frustrated. Instead of tearing up the kingdom of darkness, I was tearing off shingles. Instead of preparing sermons, I was prepping roofs. Instead of wielding God's Word in power from behind a pulpit, I was swinging a hammer at nails up on a house.

On this particular day Kenny could tell I was frustrated with myself and where I currently was in life. Sweating in the hot sun for twelve-hour days while covered in dirt and tar has a way of depleting your zest for life and ministry.

He pulled me aside and spoke words of life into my soul. He said, "Stier, I know you are called to be a preacher someday. Everyone on this roof knows you're called to be a preacher someday. But you are called to be a roofer today. So roof and do it for the glory of God, and learn every lesson he has for you during this season of life. He will use all those lessons later on. Believe me."

That less-than-a-minute pep talk changed everything for me. I began to look at every house I was roofing as the very house of Jesus. I imagined that he would come up and inspect it afterward. From that moment I allowed the roof to become my pulpit and my fellow roofers to be my congregation. I set my little Casio watch to beep every twenty minutes to remind me to get filled with the Holy Spirit. When that irritated my fellow roofers, I tied a red ribbon around my hammer wrist. The sight of the red reminded me of the blood of Jesus and my need to pray. I used every opportunity to encourage my fellow believers on the roof and evangelize the unbelieving roofers and homeowners of the homes we were roofing.

Everything changed because one thing changed: my perspective.

As I sought to bring God maximum glory despite the pain and strain, he used the trials during this time and the hard work of roofing to prepare me for his calling on my life.

I wouldn't trade my eight years of being a roofer (I ended up roofing through most of college too) for anything. God used it to teach me to work hard, not complain, share the gospel with some rough characters, disciple new believers on the roof, and put in a full day of work.

That's the way I lead in ministry now. It bleeds over into how we do our Dare 2 Share events. We don't just talk about evangelism; we do it. We don't just exegete the great commission; we execute it. Much of this put-what-you-learn-from-the-Scriptures-into-practice-now philosophy flows out of the work ethic I learned on the roof.

JESUS THE CRAFTSMAN AND BUILDER

Sometimes we forget that Jesus was in construction. According to Mark 6:3, he was a carpenter, probably joining his father Joseph in the trade and perhaps taking over the family business when his father became too old to work or passed away. As the oldest of seven or more siblings (he had four brothers and at least two sisters), the family needed his earnings to help provide for the household. He contributed to the support of his family through the hard work of being a carpenter.

The Greek word for carpenter, *tektōn*, means "craftsman" or "builder." According to Dr. Sabine R. Huebner,

> *Tektōnes* built not only roof structures for houses, but also other wooden structures such as oil mills, furniture, wagons, chariots, wheels, and also barges and boats. . . . Perhaps the carpenter also handled the production of wooden doors and windows. . . . Together with other builders, the carpenters also built towers, storage facilities, military defense walls, bridges, and siege machines.[1]

My friend Dr. Sean McDowell brings some penetrating insights about Jesus' life as a carpenter:

> Sons typically followed the profession of their fathers. Since his (step)father Joseph was a carpenter, Jesus likely learned the craft from him. Working as a carpenter was a challenging and multifaceted profession, so it probably entailed a six-year apprenticeship, which typically began sometime between 10 and 13 years of age.
>
> The life of a carpenter during the time of Jesus was quite mobile. Most carpenters traveled from construction site to construction site, along with other skilled craftsmen, and did not work primarily in their home village.
>
> Jesus may have been accustomed to leaving Nazareth and traveling to various provinces along the Sea of Galilee long before becoming a traveling preacher. From a young age, he might have traveled with Joseph throughout Galilee, working on different projects, and thus becoming familiar with the land he would eventually travel through as an adult.[2]

In the Gospels, we read nothing about Jesus during his years working as a carpenter. But we have clues and cues, from both the Old and the New Testaments, about how crucial these working years were for Jesus.

These quiet years of Jesus' carpenter life provide four insights that can help us become radical like Jesus.

JESUS LEARNED TO WORK WELL WITH OTHERS

Even if you work alone, construction is never a solo project. You work with wholesalers, contractors, and other workers, as well as with clients.

I'm sure that Jesus learned how to relate well with others during this time. He learned to ask questions and listen deeply to their answers. I can imagine him listening to stories and jokes and perhaps sharing a few himself. After all, you can tell he was a master storyteller from the parables in the Gospels. Perhaps he, like me, honed his storytelling craft while sitting around with a bunch of guys at break time, shooting the breeze.

JESUS BUILT TO THE HIGHEST OF STANDARDS

Imagine what a table that Jesus built would look like. The Amish would have nothing on him. He built to last and built for beauty. Imagine the Creator of the universe stepping back from some finished building project and silently quoting Genesis 1:31 to himself: "God saw all that he had made, and it was very good."

His work would pass any inspection, both technically and aesthetically. His roofs wouldn't leak. His walls wouldn't fall. His tables wouldn't wobble.

Jesus, the master carpenter, worked for the Master of the universe, his Father. He worked for his glory. Every building project reflected that.

Does your work reflect excellence? Do you do your work for God's glory, not just enough to pass inspection?

JESUS WAS LIKELY MOCKED AND PERSECUTED

In the world of construction, if you are a committed believer in Jesus, there's a good chance you'll get mocked. When you don't laugh at the dirty jokes or refuse to rip a client off by charging for something that's not needed or choose not to gossip or curse or complain, others will turn on you.

It happened to me countless times during my eight years as a roofer. I faltered at times. Jesus never did.

It's highly likely Jesus was mocked by his fellow workers, some of whom may have included his four younger half-brothers: James, Joseph, Judas, and Simon. Perhaps he had a reputation around town for being a Goody Two-shoes, and was ridiculed as a result.

My buddy Mark Edwards, director of Sonlife Latin America, believes Psalm 69:7-12 refers to Jesus during his growing up years in Nazareth, and I'm inclined to agree with him:

I endure scorn for your sake,
     and shame covers my face.
I am a foreigner to my own family,
     a stranger to my own mother's children;
for zeal for your house consumes me,
     and the insults of those who insult you fall on me.
When I weep and fast,
     I must endure scorn;
when I put on sackcloth,
     people make sport of me.
Those who sit at the gate mock me,
     and I am the song of the drunkards.

The disciples connected this psalm with Jesus after he cleansed the Temple the first time in John 2:17: "His disciples remembered that it is written: 'Zeal for your house will consume me.'"

Perhaps not just this verse but this entire passage is about Jesus, much of it before he came onto the public scene. If so, he was mocked by his brothers and sisters. He was mocked by those around him. When he saw their sins, he wept and fasted with sackcloth on, and how did they respond? The leaders mocked him at the city gates and the drunkards sang songs about this carpenter with a conscience.

When you work for God's glory and refuse to compromise or complain, there will be those who mock you. It happened to me as a roofer. It may have happened to Jesus as a carpenter. It will happen to you too.

JESUS DEEPENED HIS PRAYER LIFE, MASTERY OF SCRIPTURE, AND FAITH

During his years as a carpenter, Jesus undoubtedly memorized and meditated on Scripture, escaped to pray, and learned to live in a moment-by-moment declaration of dependence on the Holy Spirit. The likely hardship he faced hardened his resolve. The mockery of his brothers and fellow citizens infused sanctified steel into his spine. Instead of yielding to bitterness, he felt compassion for the lost sinners around him who desperately needed a Savior.

Are you praying while at work? Are you memorizing and meditating on Scripture? Do you seek to get filled and fueled by his Holy Spirit throughout the day? (More on this later in chapter 15.)

God uses work and the trials that go with it to grow us and prepare us for his calling in our lives. As we seek to bring him glory in our day-to-day grind, he makes us holy, humble, and hungry for him and his purposes. Work, especially hard work, is a way God prepares us for the calling ahead.

I still have my original Estwing roofing hammer. From time to time, I take it out of its drawer in my garage and just look at it to remind me of those hard years in the hot summer sun. I think of Kenny's speech to me: "You are called to be a preacher someday. But you are called to be a roofer today." And then I thank God for the privilege of being a roofer for so many years and the valuable lessons it taught me. It prepared me for my calling today.

Your hard work is doing the same.

RADICAL LIKE JESUS CHALLENGE #3
Difficulty: Easy

Pray this prayer five times during your next full workday (before work, during break, over lunch, during break, end of day), and work that day like Jesus is standing next to you, checking your motives, hearing your words, and inspecting your work.

> Dear God,
>
> May every second of my workday be sanctified for your glory today and every day. May I reflect Jesus in my actions and in my interactions with my coworkers. May I do my work for the honor of your name and with the right attitude. Instead of complaining, may I give thanks. Instead of slandering others, may I build up others. Instead of mediocre work, may I produce excellence for your maximum glory. Use my attitude and the quality of my work to draw others to yourself today. And when people ask about it, may I point them to you.
>
> In Jesus' name I pray, amen.

4

BELONG

When all the people were being baptized, Jesus was baptized too.
And as he was praying, heaven was opened and the Holy Spirit descended
on him in bodily form like a dove. And a voice came from heaven:
"You are my Son, whom I love; with you I am well pleased."

LUKE 3:21-22

HAVE YOU EVER FELT LIKE YOU DIDN'T BELONG?

My family was full of macho men, bodybuilders, street fighters, and powerlifters. Me? I was more like Young Sheldon in the hood. I didn't crack skulls; I cracked books. I didn't carry a gun; I carried a dictionary (sad but true).

I didn't fit in to my tattooed, fist-fighting, bicep-flexing family.

But on one sunny summer Sunday in 1974, I heard the gospel clearly and put my faith in Jesus. Then it clicked. I did belong after all! I belonged to God.

On the drive home from church that day with my grandparents (my mom didn't go to church), my grandma opened my little red Bible and wrote this inside the front cover: "Greg Stier received Jesus Christ as his Savior on June 23, 1974."

My newfound sense of belonging was further deepened a few weeks later when I was water baptized. The little congregation of Bethany Baptist Church was so excited. Everyone cheered for me.

My salvation experience and subsequent water baptism gave my eight-year-old self a sense of belonging for the first time in my life. From that point forward something deeply profound shifted in my life—because now I knew I had a heavenly Father who loved me, a Savior who gave his life for me, and the Holy Spirit who came to live inside me.

As believers, we are each invited in to experience this deep, soul-shaping sense of belonging that overflows from an intimate relationship with the triune God. But how do we do this? What does it look like to know this in your soul? The first step is to explore the nature of the Trinity.

THE NATURE OF THE TRINITY

While the word *Trinity* never appears in the Bible, several verses reference the concept of one God in three persons. Here's a key passage from Jesus' life:

> When all the people were being baptized, Jesus was baptized too. And as he was praying, heaven was opened and the Holy Spirit descended on him in bodily form like a dove. And a voice came from heaven: "You are my Son, whom I love; with you I am well pleased."
> LUKE 3:21-22

In these two verses we can identify the three members of the Trinity. We watch the Son getting baptized. We hear the

Father's voice. We see the Holy Spirit descending on Jesus like a dove.

This beautiful event gives us a glimpse into how the members of the Holy Trinity are in holy synergy with each other. When the Spirit of God descended on Jesus, Jesus was not only empowered for the mission that lay ahead but was also reminded that he belonged in the Trinity.

But what is the Trinity? The traditional theological definition is this: "There is one God who eternally exists as three distinct Persons—the Father, Son, and Holy Spirit."[1]

There is one God, yet three distinct persons make up that one God. But each is fully God.

Mind blown yet? You are not alone. Theologians across the millennia have been trying to make the infinite Trinity understandable to our finite human brains.

Some have used the illustration of an egg to describe the Trinity. An egg has three parts: shell, yolk, and white. One egg, three parts. Sound good? But here's where that analogy falls short. A shell by itself is not an egg. A yolk by itself is not an egg. A white by itself is not an egg. But the Father, Son, and Holy Spirit are each individually God in and of themselves. But they still are only one God comprised of three persons.

Some have used the analogy of H_2O. Water comes in three forms: ice, water, and steam. But it's all H_2O. But here's where this illustration falls short. Ice, water, and steam are really the same exact essence with no distinction other than their form. Each member of the Trinity is the same essence, but they are different in person, not just form.[2]

All human illustrations describing the Trinity that I'm familiar with fall short on some level. But there is one classic diagram that does a pretty good job of capturing the Trinity.

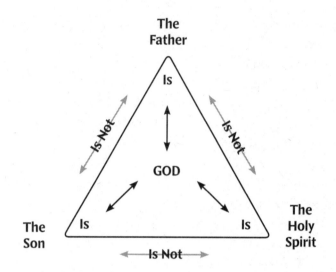

Let's start in the middle of the diagram with God. The Bible says in Deuteronomy 6:4, "Hear, O Israel: The Lord our God, the Lord is one."

This is called the *Shema* after the Hebrew for the first word ("hear"). It is the core creed of Judaism. It is a declaration to all Jews that there is only one God who is truly God.

We serve *one* God, not three. We don't just see this in the Old Testament with the *Shema*. We see it in the New Testament, for example, in Ephesians 4:4-6: "There is . . . one Lord, one faith, one baptism; one God and Father of all, who is over all and through all and in all."

UNIQUE AND DISTINCT

Each member of the Trinity is unique and distinct.

Who is the Father? He is in charge. In John 5:19 Jesus says, "The Son can do nothing by himself; he can do only what he sees his Father doing."

The Bible says in 1 Timothy 6:16 that the Father alone "lives in unapproachable light" and that no person has seen him or can see him. He is the one who makes the plans, the one who is ultimately in charge. You see this throughout the whole Old Testament.

Who is the Son? The Son is the second person of the Trinity. He is fully God and fully human and is the visible expression of the Trinity. Two thousand years ago he "emptied himself" (see Philippians 2:7) to become one of us. The Son of God became the Son of Man. He is not 50 percent human and 50 percent God. He is 100 percent human and 100 percent God and 100 percent sinless. Think about it this way: we have a human representative as a member of the Trinity. Jesus Christ will always be 100 percent human and 100 percent God and 100 percent a member of the Trinity. John 1:18 puts it this way: "No one has ever seen God, but the one and only Son, who is himself God and is in closest relationship with the Father, has made him known."

Who is the Holy Spirit? The Spirit is the third person of the Trinity, who gladly follows the lead of the Father and the Son. The Holy Spirit is the member of the Trinity who empowers us for life and service and witness (see Ephesians 5:18-19). He is the Comforter who brings us peace in times of trouble (see John 14:26). He is the one who guided the hands and hearts of the writers of the Bible so that every word written is truly the Word of God (see 2 Peter 1:20-21). It is the Holy Spirit who gives us boldness to share our faith. The last words of Jesus to his disciples were a reminder that the Spirit would empower them—and us— to evangelize: "You will receive power when the Holy Spirit comes on you; and you will be my witnesses in Jerusalem, and in all Judea and Samaria, and to the ends of the earth" (Acts 1:8).

While they are each distinct Persons with distinct roles, they all work together in holy synergy with each other. For example, they all work together to save you. God the Father chooses you. Jesus died and rose to redeem you. The Spirit regenerates you, bringing you from death to life.

Additionally, they all work together to sanctify you, to help you run the race of your life for God's glory. The Father marks out the race for you to run. The Son intercedes on your behalf and prays for you as you run. The Spirit empowers you to run.

The Father is God. The Son is God. The Holy Spirit is God. Now look at the Trinity diagram again and notice that the Father is not the Son. The Son is not the Spirit. And the Spirit is not the Father.

Yet there is a deeper level of community, love, and kinship between the members of the Trinity than we could ever imagine. They are in perfect relationship.

INVITED IN, BUT NOT MEMBERS OF

Have you ever wondered why God created humanity? Was he lonely? No, he was perfectly happy before a single angel or human ever existed. The Father loved the Son, and the Son loved the Spirit, and they all loved one another in a way we can never fully comprehend.

So why did God create humans? Perhaps the answer is that he wanted to show us his love. He wanted someone else to experience the love that each member of the Trinity has for the others.

Have you ever eaten something really good and said to someone, "Hey, taste this—it's delicious"? Perhaps God created humanity so that he could offer us his love and say, "Taste and see that the LORD is good" (Psalm 34:8).

We get a glimpse of this in John 17, when Jesus delivers a prayer to God for his disciples just hours before he was crucified. He prays this in John 17:20-21:

> My prayer is not for them alone. I pray also for those who
> will believe in me through their message [that's us], that

all of them may be one, Father, just as you are in me and I am in you. May they also be in us so that the world may believe that you have sent me.

The same unbreakable, unimaginable oneness and love the members of the Trinity have for each other is opened up to you! You get to experience unity with God! You get to experience the love the Father has for the Son and the love the Son has for the Spirit!

And, as a result, you are invited in. You are invited in through the blood of Christ, as Hebrews 10:19 declares: "And so, dear brothers and sisters, we can boldly enter heaven's Most Holy Place *because of the blood of Jesus*" (NLT, emphasis added).

Because Jesus died on the cross in your place and for your sins, you have access into the inner room of the Trinity. You are not alone. You are never alone. The Spirit of God indwelled you at the moment of salvation, and Jesus promised you the Father and Son would both make their home with you.

I'll never forget a note I received from twelve-year-old Lily after teaching on this Trinitarian truth. In it she described sitting alone at a school cafeteria table. Here's what she said in her own words:

The pain inside me had been burning my heart into ashes for years. No one knew about this pain. Not my family or friends. I had many friends, yet every day, I lived a nightmare and I felt so alone. I usually put on a mask— one of great confidence and happiness—and tried to look like I didn't have a care in the world. I succeeded in fooling everyone. No one saw past my mask. That hurt. I used to cry myself to sleep. I felt really pathetic and useless.

Lily said that she had even tried to commit suicide. But when Lily learned the radical truth that she belonged in relationship with God and was being invited into the fellowship of the Trinity, joy filled her soul. She said she imagined the Father sitting across from her at her school cafeteria and the Son and the Spirit sitting at her right and her left. She said she would never attempt suicide again because now she knew she wasn't alone.

That same truth of belonging with the Trinity can transform you as well. You are not alone. Just like Jesus, you belong.

RADICAL LIKE JESUS CHALLENGE #4
Difficulty: Easy

We are only fully empowered to live a radical life when we experience the intimacy of belonging in relationship with the Triune God. Write your name in the Trinitarian diagram and write a letter to God thanking him that you belong—that you are not a member of but are invited into the intimacy of the Trinity.

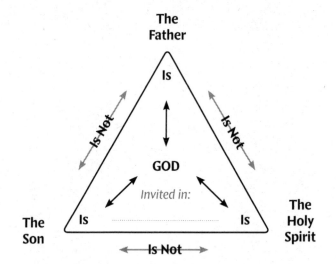

Dear God,

5

EMBRACE

A voice from heaven said,
"This is my Son, whom I love;
with him I am well pleased."

MATTHEW 3:17

DECADES AGO, Toney was a sergeant in the United States Army. He fought valiantly for God and country in the Korean War. Captured by the North Koreans, for three long years Toney was tortured and subjected to the unthinkable. Even after the Korean Armistice Agreement (the official cessation of hostilities between the United States and North Korea), he was tortured for months behind enemy lines.

Toney was the very last American POW released by the North Koreans. When he finally returned to the United States, he was a decorated war hero, having received the Prisoner of War Medal.

Toney decided to stay in the Army, but he struggled. Perhaps it was PTSD from the trauma he endured while in captivity. Whatever the reason, he turned to alcohol and partying.

One night he met a girl named Shirley. They partied. She

got pregnant. He found out. He got transferred two thousand miles away.

When he died, he left behind a few old, tarnished medals and commendations from the war, a family that didn't know his full story, and a son he had never met—me.

I am Toney's illegitimate son. He deserted me and my mom before I was ever born. I've never seen his face. I've never heard his voice.

Since I was little, down deep in my soul, there's always been a father-shaped chasm. I long to hear the words, "Well done, Son. I'm proud of you. I love you." But I've never heard that from an earthly father. And I never will.

I wonder if Jesus, too, had a father-shaped chasm of sorts. By the time of his baptism, there's a good chance that his earthly stepfather, Joseph, was already dead, maybe for many years. As the oldest child, Jesus was very likely head of the household.

Jesus had a loving mama, for sure. Mary was the best. But it may have been many years since he had heard "Well done, Son" from his earthly father.

Perhaps you can relate.

Maybe you have a dad who is a hard-driving perfectionist, where good is never good enough. Instead of hearing "Well done," you've heard a million ways a project, school assignment, job, or spouse choice could have been better.

Maybe you have a dad who is just disconnected, so into his own world of work or sports or alcohol or whatever that you feel like he doesn't even care about you.

Maybe you have a great father, one who loves you no matter what and is continually trying to encourage you.

Maybe, like me, you have no dad. You can only imagine what it would be like to have a caring father who loves you no matter what.

PIVOTAL, POWERFUL, AND PERSONAL

For Jesus, the presence and voice of his heavenly Father after his water baptism was pivotal, powerful, and ever so personal. It had been more than thirty years since he last heard his voice in heaven. Perhaps as he got up from the right side of the Father and prepared for the Incarnation, his Father said his last audible words to him. We can only imagine the intimacy of that moment.

But now Jesus heard his loving Papa's voice once again. And what did the Father say? "This is my Son . . ." The Father addressed the issue of Jesus' identity for everyone to hear. Jesus was the Son of God. For any unbeliever during that time or any doubters alive today, the Father made a clear proclamation that Jesus is truly the Son of God himself.

Jesus embraced his identity in that moment. He was his Father's Son. Of course, he was fully God, existing from eternity past, almighty and omnipotent, but in this passage he was reminded that he was not just a son, but the very Son of God himself.

And the Father expressed his love for him—days before Jesus' temptation in the desert, months before his first miracle, years before his death on the cross.

God the Father's words of love aren't because of anything Jesus had done but because of his identity. The Father loved Jesus because he was his *Son*.

I'll never forget an incident involving my own son, Jeremy. From the time he was in preschool until he graduated from high school, Jeremy attended the same Christian school. One day he came home in tears. He had broken a minor rule at school, stepping out of line during recess. He was harshly rebuked by his third-grade teacher. "Jeremy," the teacher had said, "you should be ashamed of yourself. You are a disgrace to your father."

When Jeremy told me this, I was furious. But before I lunged toward the phone to set up a meeting with the teacher and the principal, I looked at my son and said, "Jeremy, you are my son, and I love you no matter what. You are no disgrace to me."

During the tense meeting at school the next day I told the teacher, "I have worked hard to make sure my son never feels the pressure of being the son of a ministry leader and traveling evangelist. All that came tumbling down when you called my son a disgrace. So I had to reassure Jeremy of his identity as my beloved son. Never say anything like that to him again."

She didn't.

BELOVED CHILD OF GOD

Many times, Satan seeks to speak death into our souls by getting us to doubt our identity. But make no mistake, if you have put your faith in Jesus, you are a child of God.

John 1:12 makes it clear: "To all who did receive him, to those who believed in his name, he gave the right to become children of God." Think about that. Just like Jesus, you have the right to call yourself a child of God. No one can ever take that away from you.

You are as loved by the Father as Jesus was and is. Let that soak in for a moment.

The Lord loves you with an everlasting love! As with Jesus, he loved you before you did anything to please him. He loved you before you shared the gospel, went to church, gave in the offering plate, or made your first disciple. He loved you before the foundation of the earth: "He chose us in him before the creation of the world to be holy and blameless in his sight. In love he predestined us for adoption to sonship through Jesus Christ, in accordance with his pleasure and will" (Ephesians 1:4-5).

Romans 8:31-39 puts it in a way where you can't help but throw your arms up in victory:

What, then, shall we say in response to these things? If God is for us, who can be against us? He who did not spare his own Son, but gave him up for us all—how will he not also, along with him, graciously give us all things? Who will bring any charge against those whom God has chosen? It is God who justifies. Who then is the one who condemns? No one. Christ Jesus who died—more than that, who was raised to life—is at the right hand of God and is also interceding for us. Who shall separate us from the love of Christ? Shall trouble or hardship or persecution or famine or nakedness or danger or sword? . . .

No, in all these things we are more than conquerors through him who loved us. For I am convinced that neither death nor life, neither angels nor demons, neither the present nor the future, nor any powers, neither height nor depth, nor anything else in all creation, will be able to separate us from the love of God that is in Christ Jesus our Lord.

Embrace your identity as a child of God who is loved by God. Embrace it in the depth of your soul so it becomes pivotal, powerful, and personal. When you do, it will give you a holy swagger to tackle any struggle or any sin.

As a fatherless, inner-city kid raised in a crazy-violent home, it would have been easy to let the poverty, fatherlessness, or violence around me determine the script for my identity. But on the day the gospel was clearly shared with me as an eight-year-old boy, I found my identity as a child of God. It's almost as though I heard the words from heaven, "This is my son, whom I love . . ."

Soon after my conversion, I started attending the hyper-fundamentalist, super-legalistic church that reached my family for

Jesus. The legalism could have easily train-wrecked my identity for a lifetime by making it dependent on what I did for God instead of what he did for me.

But despite the struggles I had growing up in such a performance-driven culture, I was able to somehow cling to my identity as a child of God. The Triune God has been my anchor in the storm. God alone has been my firm foundation. The intense violence I witnessed growing up; the pain of being abandoned by my biological father; the shock of almost dying four times before the age of eleven; the anxiety of being raised in a high-crime area by a single, shame-fueled mom; the guilt of constantly failing to measure up to the impossible standards of a super legalistic church—all of this is *nothing* compared to the overwhelming love of God. Pain and trauma are not reasons to *reject* faith in God; they are reasons to cling that much more to the truth that you are a beloved child of God. They are reasons to run to the Father, Son, and Spirit every day.

Twenty years ago, while my ma was slowly dying in hospice over forty days and forty nights, we had many amazing conversations. One of them started with a simple question she asked me from her bed. "Do you remember what you used to say when kids from the neighborhood made fun of you for not having a dad?"

I thought for a moment and responded, "No."

Turning her penetrating blue eyes on me, she said, "You used to say, 'God's my dad.'"

"Ma," I said, "I don't remember saying that, but I remember feeling that from the moment I put my faith in Jesus."

By God's grace and through his divine intervention, I embraced my identity.

Embrace yours, too.

It's almost as though you can hear a voice from heaven declaring over you, "You are my beloved child, whom I love."

Write your name in all the blanks in the following passage from
Ephesians 1:3-14, replacing the pronouns you/we/us with your own
name:

Praise be to the God and Father of our Lord Jesus Christ,
who has blessed _____ in the heavenly realms with
every spiritual blessing in Christ. For he chose _____
in him before the creation of the world to be holy and
blameless in his sight. In love he predestined _____
for adoption to sonship through Jesus Christ, in accordance
with his pleasure and will—to the praise of his glorious
grace, which he has freely given _____ in the One
he loves. In him _____ [has] redemption through
his blood, the forgiveness of sins, in accordance with the
riches of God's grace that he lavished on _____.
With all wisdom and understanding, he made known
to _____ the mystery of his will according to his
good pleasure, which he purposed in Christ, to be put
into effect when the times reach their fulfillment—
to bring unity to all things in heaven and on earth
under Christ.

In him _____ [was] also chosen, having been
predestined according to the plan of him who works out
everything in conformity with the purpose of his will, in
order that _____ . . . might be for the praise of his
glory. And _____ also [was] included in Christ when
_____ heard the message of truth, the gospel of
_____'s salvation. When _____ believed,
_____ [was] marked in him with a seal, the promised

Holy Spirit, who is a deposit guaranteeing _____'s inheritance until the redemption of those who are God's possession—to the praise of his glory.

#

6

Jesus said to him, "Away from me, Satan! For it is written:
'Worship the Lord your God, and serve him only.'"
MATTHEW 4:10

HAVE YOU EVER BEEN IN A FIGHT? Maybe it was in elementary school and the school bully set their eyes on you. They taunted you and mocked you until enough was enough. Before you knew it, you pushed back, and the fight was on.

Although I came from a fighting family, I was not a fighter. I'd run like Forrest Gump long before I'd punch like Rocky Balboa. They were bold as lions; I was meek as a mouse. As a result of my shyness, bookishness, and fear of fighting, many in my rough-and-tumble family thought something was wrong with me.

During my elementary school years, the whole family frequently gathered at Uncle Jack (the toughest of my tough uncles) and Aunt Earlene's house. While talking to a table full of family members, Uncle Jack looked over at me and said, "What's wrong with that kid? He reads books."

All of this played into my psyche. It felt like somebody forgot to pour a cupful of testosterone into my genes. I wondered if I had any of their tough-guy DNA at all. But years later something happened that forever changed my mind.

We had moved out from "the bad part of town" into the suburbs, and I was a high schooler at Arvada Christian School.

At this small school our gym classes were pretty intense—so intense that one month out of the year, all the high school guys were matched up to box. After all, nothing says, "Be more like Jesus" than two teenagers strapping on headgear and gloves and trying to knock each other out—for the glory of God.

When the dreaded time came to see who I would be matched with, my heart dropped. I was matched with Salazar. (He called me Stier, and I called him Salazar, although, jokingly, I sometimes called him "Salad Bar").

Here was the problem. Salazar, too, was from the streets, and he actually knew how to box. The rumor floating around our school was that he had been trained by a Golden Gloves boxer. And to add insult to a highly likely injury, he outweighed me by twenty pounds.

Maybe I shouldn't have called him "Salad Bar" after all.

Our match was set for Friday, and I had all week to prepare. But instead of getting fighting tips from my uncles, aunts, and cousins, I did what any teenager trying to learn how to box in a week would do in the early eighties.

I rented the movie *Rocky* and watched it every night.

Mimicking the moves, I shadowboxed in my basement and imagined I was Rocky Balboa and Salazar was my own personal Apollo Creed.

On Friday, all the high school boys sat in a big circle as duo after duo was called up to box three three-minute rounds. Finally,

Salazar and I were called up to fight. I remember nervously putting on the headgear and regulation-sized gloves.

The whole time I was reminding myself, *Okay, jab, bob, and weave. Stay light on your feet. Just keep jabbing, keep dancing, keep moving . . . just like Rocky.*

I noticed that all during this time, Salazar just stood there smiling a smile of self-confident victory.

Right before our gym teacher, Timo, sent us into the middle of the "ring," a terrifying thought hit me like an uppercut. *There's no way I'm going to win this fight. He is trained, and I am not. I got my training from a movie. He got his training from a real boxer. He is bigger than me, and he knows what he's doing. I'm going to get killed.*

But like a thunder boom following a lightning bolt, a very different thought struck my brain. *Yes, he can box. But he can't box without a head. If I knock his head off, he won't be able to hit back.*

Suddenly I knew what I had to do.

When the fight officially started, I swung my right fist so hard and hit him in the side of the head with such force that his headgear completely turned around and covered his eyes. I knew this was my chance, so I jumped on him like a spider monkey and swung away—in the name of Jesus, for the glory of God.

He fell to the ground, and I continued to pummel him until Timo pulled me off.

I may or may not have been drooling at the time.

After he shakily got up from the ground, I just chased him around our makeshift ring saying, "I'm hungry, Salad Bar. I'm hungry."

What did I discover that day? I discovered that I could fight after all. Maybe I *did* belong in my family.

You can fight too. And you come from a family of fighters, a spiritual family.

As a matter of fact, Jesus, our spiritual big brother (see Hebrews 2:11), was the true ultimate fighter. He didn't fight with his fists. He fought with his words. He fought with God's Word. Three of the Gospels describe a fight Jesus had with Satan in the wilderness.

In Luke 4:1-2 we read, "Jesus, full of the Holy Spirit, left the Jordan and was led by the Spirit into the wilderness, where for forty days he was tempted by the devil. He ate nothing during those days, and at the end of them he was hungry."

Satan knew if he could get Jesus to sin, his death on the cross would be meaningless, because only a perfect sacrifice could satisfy God's wrath for the sins of humanity (see Hebrews 10:12).

That's when Satan started throwing his punches, seeking to knock him out as the perfect sacrifice by tempting him to sin.

PUNCH #1: A JAB AT JESUS' IDENTITY

The devil said to him, "If you are the Son of God, tell these stones to become bread" (Matthew 4:3).

At first glance this temptation was about food. After all, Jesus was hungry after forty days of fasting in the wilderness, and who doesn't love piping hot breadsticks? But on a deeper level, this attack was on his identity—"If you are the Son of God . . ."

In a similar way, how often does Satan take a jab at your identity as a believer? He calls you sinner, although God calls you saint (see Romans 1:7). He calls you loser, although God calls us "more than conquerors" (Romans 8:37). He calls you worthless, although God calls us sons and daughters (see Galatians 3:26).

PUNCH #2: AN UPPERCUT AT JESUS' SENSE OF BELONGING

Then the devil took him to the holy city and had him stand on the highest point of the temple. "If you are

the Son of God," he said, "throw yourself down. For it
is written:

"'He will command his angels concerning you,
    and they will lift you up in their hands,
    so that you will not strike your foot against a stone.'"
MATTHEW 4:5-6

You can see the attack on Jesus' identity again in this passage
with the same seven words: "If you are the Son of God . . ." But
you also can see an attack on his belonging. Here's my paraphrase
of Satan's challenge to Jesus: "If you really belong as a member of
the Trinity, then the Father will dispatch angels to capture you if
you jump off the high point of the Temple. Before you hit the
ground and go splat, God will send his angelic spotters to set you
down gently. Then everyone worshipping in the Temple will know
you belong to the Trinity."

Many times Satan attacks our sense of belonging too. Have you
ever felt like you don't fit into the body of Christ or that you have
no true community? Often these are the flaming lies of the evil
one shot like an arrow straight at your heart, thrown like a boxer's
uppercut straight at your chin.

But you *do* belong. Ephesians 2:19-20 makes this abundantly
clear: "Consequently, you are no longer foreigners and strangers,
but fellow citizens with God's people and also members of his
household, built on the foundation of the apostles and prophets,
with Christ Jesus himself as the chief cornerstone."

PUNCH #3: A LEFT HOOK AT JESUS' PURPOSE

Many boxing fans consider the left hook the most powerful punch
in boxing. This is what Satan throws at Jesus in Matthew 4:8-9:

"Again, the devil took him to a very high mountain and showed him all the kingdoms of the world and their splendor. 'All this I will give you,' he said, 'if you will bow down and worship me.'"

This is a direct assault on Jesus' purpose. Satan is offering Jesus a crown without a cross, the glorious throne without the painful groans, the "hails" without the nails. Satan is offering Jesus a shortcut to the earthly kingdom, one without a trail of blood behind him.

How many times does Satan offer you shortcuts? If you just lie, you can get that promotion more quickly. If you just cheat, you can get more money faster. If you just exaggerate, you'll look more impressive without putting in the hard work.

But Satan is a big fat liar. Here's what Jesus says about him in John 8:44: "He was a murderer from the beginning, not holding to the truth, for there is no truth in him. When he lies, he speaks his native language, for he is a liar and the father of lies." From the time he possessed a serpent in the Garden of Eden until the time he will oppress believers during the Tribulation, lying is his language. He speaks in a dialect of deceit and has an infatuation with fabrication.

Satan's shortcuts are always cul-de-sacs.

However, Jesus didn't just bob and weave to avoid Satan's punches. He counterpunched. Three different times Satan threw furious fists of utter rage at Jesus. Three different times Jesus punched back with Scripture.

"It is written . . ."

"It is written . . ."

"It is written . . ."

Jesus quoted verses from the Old Testament that counteracted the lies Satan was throwing at him. And Satan eventually threw in the towel.

What's the lesson?

We must, like Jesus, memorize passages of Scripture and always be ready to counterpunch his lies. Again, Jesus wasn't born with the Old Testament memorized (and the New Testament wasn't written until after he ascended into heaven). No, he had to go through the line-by-line repetition of Bible verses when he was young, just like all the other Jewish kids. Just like we must when we memorize verses.

If you want to live like Jesus lived, you must do what Jesus did. And Jesus memorized large portions of Scripture (some say the entire Old Testament) so he could meditate on it and use it as brass knuckles when Satan showed up.

ARMOR ON, BATTLE READY

In Ephesians 6:10-17, the apostle Paul uses a different analogy than a counterpunch to represent the Word of God. After framing the Christian life as a spiritual fight, he lists the individual pieces of spiritual armor available to every believer in Ephesians, capping it off in verse 17: "Take the helmet of salvation and the sword of the Spirit, which is the word of God." Scripture is clearly a key offensive weapon against Satan and his army of demons.

In the Greek, there are two primary words for "word": *logos* and *rhema*. The word *logos* can be applied to the written word (like the Bible), but the word *rhema* means "spoken word."

The Greek word used in Ephesians 6:17 to describe God's Word is the lesser-used *rhema*. How do you use God's "spoken word" to fight against Satan? Easy. You speak it. This assumes that you've memorized enough relevant Bible verses to counteract specific temptations of the devil—just like Jesus did.

Whether it's downloading a good Bible verse memory app (like Verses) or purchasing the Topical Memory System from the legends of verse memorization, the Navigators, or just going old school with three-by-five cards (verse on one side, reference on the other), do something to start memorizing verses. For standing against some of the evil one's most common lies and temptations, I recommend starting with the following ten selections. To counterpunch . . .

- doubting your salvation, memorize John 10:28
- anxiety and worry, memorize Philippians 4:6-7
- lust, memorize 1 John 2:15-16
- pride, memorize James 4:10
- self-image problems, memorize Psalm 139:13-14
- shame over past sins, memorize Colossians 2:13-14
- bitterness toward someone who hurt you, memorize Ephesians 4:32
- the fear of death, memorize Hebrews 2:14-15
- negative, destructive thoughts, memorize Philippians 4:8
- anger toward others, memorize James 1:19

Just like Satan tried to take Jesus out by attacking his identity, belonging, and purpose, he will try to knock you out in these three areas and then some. You must punch back by memorizing Scripture verses, standing on those truths, and quoting them out loud when Satan attacks.

When you have biblical truths embedded deep in your heart and mind, it radically changes how you react when facing challenging situations. You'll be equipped to stand and fight—not in the ways of the world but in the way of Jesus.

RIOTSTARTERS: TAKING A RADICAL STAND FOR JESUS

Jerrod Gunter, a youth pastor in Memphis, Tennessee, is a prime example of standing and fighting Jesus' way. Jerrod drove up to his youth campus one morning to find the front lawn covered with crime scene tape. A white police officer had shot and killed a young black man there the night before.

Many of his students knew this young man. They were angry, filled with questions, and searching for answers. Some in their communities were urging them to join the riots that had broken out in the city.

Jerrod's pastor asked him to preach the following Sunday since it was a teenager who died on their church property. The tension was palpable that Sunday morning. Memphis had been a powder keg anyway. With active gangs, a high murder rate, and growing tension between the police and the young people, this looked like a spark that could make the city explode. The rage was ready to overflow.

That Sunday Jerrod gathered his courage as he got up to preach. "How many of you are angry a cop shot this young man on our church property?" he asked.

A chorus of "Amens!" rang out.

"How many of you want to do something about it?" he asked, this time with more force. The sanctuary echoed with even louder shouts of "Amen" and "Yes, preacher."

"How many of you are ready to tear this city up and burn this city down?" he bellowed. By this time, the congregation was cheering.

Then he did something radical like Jesus.

He flipped it.

"I am too," he said. After a long pause, he asked, "But what did Jesus say?" Jerrod let the question sink in. "Jesus said to forgive that cop."

The crowd was stunned. A few brave souls mumbled, "Amen."

"Jesus said to tear down strongholds, not burn down the city." The amens got louder.

"Jesus said to unite the churches of the city and take it back one block at a time." At this point the congregation was fully with him.

"Jesus said to bring a gospel solution to a social problem." Cheers erupted, and Riotstarter was unofficially born.

Jerrod challenged the church and his students to take a different stand—a radical stand. A stand for Jesus. Instead of succumbing to the temptation to take their anger to the streets and riot, he challenged them to take prayer and evangelism to their schools and communities.

Over the summer Jerrod equipped the students in his youth group to pray, care, and share. He trained them to share their faith and ready themselves for going back to school with the message and mission of Jesus.

Four hundred teenagers gathered at one school in Memphis the following September for See You at the Pole. But they didn't just meet at the flagpole once; they met weekly around the pole and prayed for revival. They prayed for their broken city.

Jerrod fought against Satan's temptation to start a real riot and decided to start a righteous one instead. When Satan tempted him to strike back, Jerrod counterpunched with turning the other cheek from Matthew 5:39. When Satan tempted Jerrod to return evil for evil, Jerrod threw the uppercut of Romans 12:19: "Do not take revenge, my dear friends, but leave room for God's wrath."

Today, years later, Riotstarter—the ministry birthed during Jerrod's powerful Sunday sermon—is making a difference. Churches across east Memphis are unifying around a gospel solution. In a sense, a gospel gang has risen up. This includes prayer protests that happen across the city, where teenagers march for justice and pray for their city block by block, sharing Jesus along the way. Teenagers have started campus clubs where hard issues are discussed and teens are equipped by other teens to evangelize.

Jerrod and his crew refuse to turn a blind eye to the injustices around them. But they have decided to take a Jesus approach. Their teenagers meet with police officers and government officials to build relationships and counterpunch the "us versus them" mentality Satan wants to incite. Jerrod understands that changed policies flow out of changed minds and changed hearts.

Jerrod knows and believes the words of Henry David Thoreau: "There are a thousand hacking at the branches of evil to one who is striking at the root." These riotstarters are striking at the root of evil and, in the process, punching Satan in the throat.

Now, years later, other urban churches have caught wind of the movement and are starting to assemble, pray, strategize, and put the radical ways of Jesus into practice. They won't stop until every teen in every city has every last chance to experience the Good News of Jesus, knowing that justice and righteousness will flow like two mighty rivers out of converted hearts and transformed minds.

May we be riotstarters against the forces of darkness. May we, like Jerrod, learn to counterpunch with a gospel solution. May we learn to be radical like Jesus by striking back against Satan with the straight-up Word of God.

RADICAL LIKE JESUS CHALLENGE #6
Difficulty: Medium

Download a good Bible verse memory app (like Verses) or purchase the Topical Memory System from the Navigators, or just use three-by-five cards (verse on one side, reference on the other), but choose three of the ten topics listed on page 60 and memorize the corresponding Bible verse(s). Be ready to fight back by saying, "It is written . . ." and then quoting Scripture out loud the next time Satan attacks you.

PURIFY

When it was almost time for the Jewish Passover, Jesus went up to
Jerusalem. In the temple courts he found people selling cattle, sheep and
doves, and others sitting at tables exchanging money. So he made a whip
out of cords, and drove all from the temple courts, both sheep and cattle;
he scattered the coins of the money changers and overturned their tables.
To those who sold doves he said, "Get these out of here! Stop turning my
Father's house into a market!" His disciples remembered that it is written:
"Zeal for your house will consume me."

JOHN 2:13-17

NOTHING BLOWS AWAY the stereotypical six-foot-tall, skinny, peace-loving, almost-a-hippie image of Jesus than his cleansing of the Temple.

Jesus actually cleansed the Temple twice. The Gospel of John describes the first occasion, near the beginning of Jesus' ministry, soon after he turned water into wine. The second instance—described in Matthew, Mark, and Luke—happened near the end of Jesus' earthly ministry, during his final Passover week.

These bookend Temple-purifying events shocked the crowds who were flooding Jerusalem for the Passover celebration. In Jesus' day, the population of Jerusalem was roughly 55,000, but during Passover week, it "could swell to 180,000."[1] Jesus' table-flipping, whip-flinging, cattle-kicking, coin-throwing, merchant-terrifying actions were no doubt the talk of the town.

Jesus wasn't just angry; he was furious. He wasn't just upset; he was enraged.

And this wasn't a knee-jerk reaction. John's account tells us, "He made a whip out of cords" (John 2:15). Jesus was righteously enraged but strategically calculated in his response.

Why? And what do his decisive actions have to do with you?

ECHOES OF EXODUS

Why was Jesus so righteously enraged by the money changers in the Temple courts?

For generations Jewish men were required to go to Jerusalem three times every year for the major religious festivals. Often these men were accompanied by their families, as when Jesus traveled with his family to the Passover celebration in Jerusalem as a twelve-year-old (see Luke 2:41-44).

The Passover feast was a powerful symbolic remembrance of the events described in Exodus 12. The firstborn sons of all the Egyptians were slaughtered by the destroying angel dispatched by God. Yet when the angel saw the blood of the lamb sacrifice painted on the Israelites' doorposts, judgment and death "passed over" their homes and their firstborn sons lived. As a result of this last and worst of the ten plagues God poured out on Egypt, the Israelites were finally free to make an exodus out of slavery and begin their long and arduous trek into the Promised Land.

After their exodus, the Passover meal was commemorated annually. Each year a young lamb was sacrificed and roasted. Along with bitter herbs and unleavened bread, the lamb was eaten on Passover night in remembrance of the hasty meal the Israelites had eaten the night they fled from Egypt. Following the feast day, the Jews would follow the commands in Exodus 12:19-20: "For seven days no yeast is to be found in your houses. And anyone, whether foreigner or native-born, who eats anything with yeast in it must be cut off from the community of Israel. Eat nothing made with yeast. Wherever you live, you must eat unleavened bread."

Leading up to Passover, Jewish families scrubbed from their house any trace of leaven (yeast). Then for the seven days following the Passover meal, they celebrated the Feast of Unleavened Bread and kept their house completely cleansed from leaven.

Leaven in Scripture often represents sin. For example, in 1 Corinthians 5:8 Paul writes, "Let us keep the Festival, not with the old bread leavened with malice and wickedness, but with the unleavened bread of sincerity and truth."

There's a foreshadowing here between the Passover ritual and the Messiah. Passover was a visual and visceral picture of the coming of Jesus. When he died on the cross, he was our ultimate sacrificial lamb. When we put our faith in him, the blood of his sacrifice is painted on the doorposts of our heart and eternal judgment passes over us. This is our own personal and powerful exodus out of sin and Satan's domain into the promised land of God's eternal Kingdom.

Now those of us who have been "passed over" for judgment through the finished work of Christ are called to scrub and scour the leaven of ongoing sin from our lives. We can walk in purity because of our ultimate purification. Because Jesus declared us righteous through our faith in him based on his finished work on the cross, we can choose to walk in victory over sin through Christ. As Romans 6:1-2 reminds us, "What shall we say, then? Shall we go on sinning so that grace may increase? By no means! We are those who have died to sin; how can we live in it any longer?"

ZEAL UNHINGED

When Jesus walked into the Temple courts both near the beginning of his earthly ministry (see John 2:13-17) and near the end (see Matthew 21:12-17; Mark 11:15-19; Luke 19:45-48), he saw sinful behavior ("leaven") everywhere.

The money changers, and most likely the Jewish religious leaders, were raking in exorbitant profits from the Jews and God-fearing Gentiles flooding in from across the Roman Empire and beyond. "Dirty Gentile money" had to be exchanged for Temple-approved Jewish coins. Of course, there was a hiked-up exchange rate. (If you've changed your money for foreign currency when entering a new country, you can relate). Then the Jews had to purchase a lamb or cow (if they were well off) or a dove (if they were poor) to make the required sacrifice in the Temple. These, too, were marked up so high, it would make Whole Foods blush.

Jesus looked around and saw greed and extortion. This was not capitalism; it was robbery. These money-grubbers had turned the Temple from a "house of prayer" into a "den of thieves."

So Jesus made a whip and cast them out.

Think about that feat. If there were nearly two hundred thousand people in Jerusalem for the feast, then there had to be hundreds, if not thousands, exchanging money for Temple-approved coins and selling Temple-approved sacrifices. This was not Jesus emptying a store of a few merchants. This was Jesus emptying a busy mall of all the salespeople on a busy Saturday afternoon! Imagine Jesus flipping tables, screaming judgment, and bringing his homemade whip onto sheep and cattle butts and perhaps a few human backs.

John 2:17 gives us some insight into what happened later: "His disciples remembered that it is written: 'Zeal for your house will consume me.'" Jesus had a zeal for the house of God. He did not let it stay corrupted. He acted—and acted decisively.

His zeal is reminiscent of Phinehas, a priest in the Old Testament. While the Israelites were wandering in the wilderness after being delivered from the Egyptians, "the men began to indulge in sexual immorality with Moabite women, who invited them to the sacrifices to their gods. The people ate the sacrificial meal and bowed down before these gods" (Numbers 25:1-2).

God poured out a plague in judgment upon them. Many of the Israelites mourned before the Lord. But some were still living in flagrant sin, eating the leaven of lust and participating in idolatry.

It all came to a screeching halt through one final, zealous act by Phinehas the priest:

> Then an Israelite man brought into the camp a Midianite woman right before the eyes of Moses and the whole assembly of Israel while they were weeping at the entrance to the tent of meeting. When Phinehas son of Eleazar, the son of Aaron, the priest, saw this, he left the assembly, took a spear in his hand and followed the Israelite into the tent. He drove the spear into both of them, right through the Israelite man and into the woman's stomach. Then the plague against the Israelites was stopped; but those who died in the plague numbered 24,000.
>
> NUMBERS 25:6-9

The plague stopped because Phinehas acted. Afterward we find God's opinion of this sold-out servant of God:

> The LORD said to Moses, "Phinehas son of Eleazar, the son of Aaron, the priest, has turned my anger away from the Israelites. Since he was as zealous for my honor among them as I am, I did not put an end to them in my zeal. Therefore tell him I am making my covenant of peace with him. He and his descendants will have a covenant of a lasting priesthood, because he was

zealous for the honor of his God and made atonement
for the Israelites."

NUMBERS 25:10-13

It was this Phinehas brand of zeal that pumped through the
veins of the Son of God, the ultimate high priest. Jesus didn't use
a spear; he used a whip. Jesus didn't stop a plague that attacked
the body; he was stopping the plague of sin that attacked the soul.

Why did Jesus cast out the money changers? Because he was
zealous for the honor of his Father among them! He could not
tolerate the sight of the holy Temple of his Father being corrupted
by sin.

What do Jesus' actions in cleansing the Temple have to do with
you? More than you might think.

Consider these words from the apostle Paul:

Do you not know that your bodies are temples of the
Holy Spirit, who is in you, whom you have received from
God? You are not your own; you were bought at a price.
Therefore honor God with your bodies.

I CORINTHIANS 6:19-20

We must make a whip and drive out of ourselves anything that
dishonors God. We must drive a spear through our lust. We must
flip over the tables of apathy and pride. We must drive out the
money changers of greed.

You and I are temples of the Holy Spirit of God. We must
honor him and keep his house clean. It's time to scour our houses
for leaven. It's time to scrub secret sins from our lives in light of
the ultimate Passover Lamb, Jesus himself.

But sometimes it's hard to see all our secret sins. What the Jews
had grown accustomed to over time, Jesus saw with holy eyes.

What is it going to take for us to see the secret sins of our souls with the eyes of Phinehas and Jesus . . . and then act with zeal to rid ourselves of it?

THE STORY OF JOSH

Years ago, I was invited to speak to about sixty high school teenagers at a weekend youth retreat. These teenagers were upper middle class and somewhat smug. In my first sermon on Friday night, I got the distinct impression that they didn't really feel the need for Jesus to save them from their sins, because they didn't see themselves as sinners. As I preached, I got a lot of rolling eyes and heavy sighs from these too-cool-for-Sunday-school students.

Instead of flipping over tables or breaking out a whip, I racked my brain for something equally radical that would help them realize they were sinners in need of a Savior.

That next day I was praying and conspiring over my radical sermon for the coming night. Then I met Josh. Josh was new to the student group. He had a drama background, and the other teenagers in the group didn't know him very well.

When Josh told me about his drama background, a thought hit me, a thought so radical I knew it would shake the other teenagers to their core—if it worked. So Josh and I brainstormed. He was excited to participate.

This idea was so edgy that I called together a spontaneous gathering of the other youth leaders and sponsors to get their permission. They hesitantly agreed.

So that night I preached on Judgment Day. I said, "Someday, we will stand before God on Judgment Day. According to 2 Corinthians 5:10, on that day we'll give an account for everything we have done, 'whether good or bad.'"

The students, just like the night before, were unimpressed.

So I continued: "But that doesn't scare most of you. Judgment Day seems way in the future, and you're not too worried about it. So tonight, I thought I'd bring Judgment Day to you."

Everybody started getting a little nervous because I had my crazy eyes going.

"I have the spiritual gift of prophecy," I said. "According to 1 Corinthians 14:24-25, when a prophet prophesies, the unbelievers will be 'convicted of sin and are brought under judgment by all, as the secrets of their hearts are laid bare. So they will fall down and worship God, exclaiming, 'God is really among you!'"

"I have the gift of prophecy!" I declared again. "I have the ability to pray over each of you individually and see which sins you struggle with. So tonight, I'm going to place this chair up here, and one by one I'm going to prophesy over you and call out the sins you struggle with. The secrets of your hearts are about to be laid bare for all to see! We are going to have our own little Judgment Day tonight!"

A nervous hush fell over the room.

I pointed to the teenager on my far right and said, "What's your name?"

"Josh," he said. (Remember: he was the plant!)

"You're up first," I said. "Come and sit in this chair."

He squirmed in his seat. "No, thank you," he said.

I pointed my finger right at him and yelled with a thunder that would make a Pentecostal preacher proud. "If you don't come up and sit in this chair, I'm kicking you out of this camp!"

Immediately everyone went from nervous to scared because they had never seen this side of me.

Josh hesitantly shuffled up to the stage and sheepishly slumped onto the chair.

I put my hand on his head and prayed, "Lord, show me his sins. Show them to me right now, in the name of Jesus!" (For whatever reason I started speaking in a Southern accent.)

Then I looked at him and said, "You struggle with drug use, don't you?"

He looked up at me and defiantly declared, "I do not!"

I brought the volume of my voice up even more and asked, "Josh, tell me the truth. Do you struggle with drugs?"

Again, he said, "No."

"BEFORE GOD, ARE YOU A DRUG USER?" I yelled.

"Yes!" he yelled back. Then he started crying with big tears rolling down his cheeks.

Josh was a great actor.

At that moment, I knew I had the crowd, because everyone else started crying too. They weren't crying for Josh. They were crying for themselves because they were convinced I would reveal their sins too.

One after another, I announced Josh's sins. When I finally got through the list, I asked him, "How do you feel? Your sins have been confessed before everyone!"

He stood up in anger, his shirt stained by the tears that were still falling off his cheeks and stuck his finger in my chest. "How do you think I feel?" he shouted. "You've ruined my life!"

He screamed as he ran down the middle aisle, pushed open the two wooden doors, and disappeared into the night.

That wasn't scripted. I had no idea he was going to run. I had no idea he was such a good actor. So I just kept going with it.

I looked at the other teens with the piercing, crazy eyes of an Elijah and declared, "You see what judgment does to wimps? Tonight, Judgment Day has come!" Then pointing at individual teens in the audience, I yelled, "And you and you and you are all gonna sit in this chair and get your sins exposed!"

Then something else happened that was not planned. A teenage boy on the front row stood up and said, "I'm out of here, dude!" and he ran down the aisle toward the chapel exit.

"Stop!" I yelled. "Wait a minute!"

He pivoted mid–reverse altar call and yelled, "What is going on?"

I came clean to him and everyone. "I don't have the gift of prophecy," I confessed. "That was all a setup. Josh was just acting. I was just trying to make a point. I repeat, I do not have the gift of prophecy, and I'm not going to reveal your sins."

And, boy, did those teens worship that night. "He ain't got the gift! Hallelujah! He ain't got the gift!"

By the way, if you are a youth leader, don't ever try this. I got in so much trouble when I got back, and I now realize this is not the best way to get teens to recognize their sins.

Although I would never do something like that again, I did make my point in a powerful way. Every teenager in the room that night was asking themselves, *What sin would I be most embarrassed by?*

So I ask you the same question: What secret sins would you be most embarrassed by if they were publicly confessed? If Jesus showed up in all his glory, what tables would he be flipping in your soul?

Under the New Covenant, *you* are the temple of God. *You* are the dwelling place of the Holy Spirit. Purify your temple. Scour it for leaven. Sweep it for sin.

What is that sin?

RADICAL LIKE JESUS CHALLENGE #7
Difficulty: Medium

Identify that one secret sin that you would be most embarrassed by if Jesus were to show up in all his glory and make your sins public. Then call up or meet with a trusted Christian friend and confess it to them. As someone once said, "We confess to God for forgiveness. But we confess to each other for healing." Confession of sin to a trusted Christian friend doesn't ruin our lives; it ruins our sins. It takes them out of the darkness and into the light where they have no more secret power over us.

Confess your sins to each other and pray for each other so that you may be healed.
JAMES 5:16

8

LOVE

God so loved the world that he gave his one and only Son,
that whoever believes in him shall not perish but have eternal life.

JOHN 3:16

ROSARIA CHAMPAGNE HAD HAD ENOUGH. Promise Keepers (PK) was coming to host a stadium event for Christian men in Syracuse, New York, where she was a well-respected, tenured university professor of English and Women's Studies. As a proud lesbian and passionate feminist, Rosaria viewed PK as antithetical to everything just and good. PK founder Coach Bill McCartney's vocal stance against homosexuality as an "abomination" was an abomination to her and all she stood for and with.

Promise Keepers was (and still is) bold in its stance for traditional marriage, contending that homosexual activity is outside God's blueprint for human sexuality. But PK's speakers—which I have been privileged to be among—spoke just as boldly about loving the lost as they did about standing for truth. Despite that, Coach McCartney's quote about homosexuality being an abomination was all that many in the public heard. It became a rallying cry for the LGBTQ community in the late nineties and catalyzed a movement against all things Promise Keepers.

Rosaria, named after the rosary, was raised as a Catholic and experienced a heterosexual adolescence. But as she moved into her twenties, she had a stronger and stronger affinity with and for her female friends. By her late twenties she identified as lesbian. Having earned her PhD, she eventually moved to New York and became a professor at Syracuse University. Although she never intended to become a gay-rights activist, she began writing a book on the religious right and what many interpreted as their politics of hatred toward those who identified as homosexual.

In anticipation of PK "invading" her city, Rosaria wrote an op-ed for the local Syracuse newspaper, *The Post-Standard*. Here are a few things she had to say:

> Bill McCartney, former coach of the University of Colorado football team, founder and CEO of the Promise Keepers . . . founded the Promise Keepers with these words: "Homosexuality is an abomination of Almighty God." Regardless of your position on gay rights, Christianity opposes the kind of hate and bigotry these words portend.
>
> While the Promise Keepers may be very useful in turning around the lives of individual men, their message and vision for the future are ultimately unhelpful for women, children and anti-racist activism and are downright bad for democracy.[1]

When her opinion piece about the coming Promise Keepers event was published, she received a flood of responses, some extremely positive and others super negative. After she read each letter, Rosaria put it into one of two piles, fan mail or hate mail. In short order, both piles were getting bigger and bigger.

But one day, a letter showed up that confounded her. She didn't know which pile to put it in. This letter was from a local pastor, Ken Smith of the Syracuse Reformed Presbyterian Church. His letter was kind and thoughtful. He didn't argue with Rosaria. He didn't accuse her of committing an abomination. Instead, he encouraged her to read the Bible and get familiar with the real Jesus who entered human history and made such a deep and lasting impact.

Rosaria didn't know how to respond to him or his letter, so she threw it away.

Ken had convictions, that was clear. But one of those convictions was love. Ken believed that we, as Christians, should self-identify as lovers of everyone, especially those we differ with on moral, cultural, and spiritual issues.

Ken and his wife, Floy, invited Rosaria to dinner, and she eventually accepted their invitation. She couldn't get Ken's compelling letter out of her head. And it wasn't just a one and well-done dinner. This dynamically dedicated duo of holy hospitality invited her back again . . . and again . . . and again. Over the course of two years, she ate regularly at their dinner table. They didn't share the gospel and invite her to say the sinner's prayer at that first dinner. They didn't invite her to church.

But they did invite her to continue the conversation.

In her words, she "never felt like a project." Instead, she felt like a neighbor and a friend. Eventually, Rosaria, at Ken and Floy's urging, started to read the Bible for herself. And she read it like a PhD would—intellectually, logically, and relentlessly.

Because God's Word is "alive and active" and "sharper than any double-edged sword" (Hebrews 4:12), it started cutting through her defenses and impacting her soul. As a professor of

English, she was impressed with the book from a literary perspective. It was packed full of poetry, prose, parables, and power. But as a learner, she was even more impressed. The book spoke with authority.

Pastor Ken kept pointing Rosaria to Jesus. And she couldn't escape him, no matter how hard she tried.

Finally, Rosaria came to church and eventually put her faith in Christ. As time went on, Rosaria concluded she couldn't be a fully devoted follower of Christ and keep pursuing a lesbian lifestyle. Under deep conviction from God's Word, she made the heart-wrenching decision to leave the woman she loved to fully serve the King who loved her exponentially more.

Today, Rosaria Champagne Butterfield is married to Kent, a Reformed Presbyterian pastor in North Carolina. She is a home-school mother, an author, and a much sought-after speaker. (You can read more about Rosaria's story in her book *The Secret Thoughts of an Unlikely Convert.*)

What reached her? It was the explosive nitroglycerin combination of truth and love. She received the truth from her intensive study of the Bible, reading it through seven times. But before that, she received love from Ken and Floy, a pastor and his wife who showered her with radical hospitality and non-accusatory love. Ken and Floy were the living personification of the first six words of John 3:16: "For God so loved the world . . ."

Jesus gave no asterisk to this claim. Jesus didn't say, "For God so loved the world . . . except the gays" or "except the murderers" or "except the anyones"! God loves the world and everyone in it.

Jesus showed this love to the religious as well as the rebellious. He showed it to a spiritually curious Jewish religious leader in John 3, a woman with a checkered past in John 4, and a proud rich man in Mark 10.

INTRIGUING LOVE

This love was demonstrated to Nicodemus in John 3 through a challenge that intrigued his theological mind: "Very truly I tell you, no one can see the kingdom of God unless they are born again" (John 3:3). This brain-straining comment threw Nicodemus the Pharisee for a loop and sent him down the righteous rabbit hole of what it meant to be born again. Right when his brain was about to blow a theological gasket trying to comprehend what it meant to be "born again," Jesus gave Nicodemus his clearest, most succinct explanation of the gospel: "For God so loved the world that he gave his one and only Son, that whoever believes in him shall not perish but have eternal life" (John 3:16).

Although we don't know whether Nicodemus ever put his faith in Jesus, it seems likely that he did. After all, he risked his status as a Pharisee when he helped give Jesus a proper burial after his crucifixion (see John 19:38-39).

It all started with a simple, intriguing statement: "You must be born again." It all started with an act of love.

Jesus used a powerful declaration to show his love to Nicodemus. One chapter later he used a simple question to demonstrate his love to the Samaritan woman. While standing without a bucket by a water well, he met this woman, known for her many past marriages and her current living-in-sin situation. He asked her, "Will you give me a drink?" (John 4:7).

Shocked by the fact that he actually talked to her, she responded, "'You are a Jew and I am a Samaritan woman. How can you ask me for a drink?' (For Jews do not associate with Samaritans)" (John 4:9).

This talk of water intrigued her and triggered a flood of conversation—about Living Water, sin, faith, and forgiveness. Soon that flood became a tsunami as the woman at the well became the woman saved from hell. Amazed, she ran into the city of Sychar to bring others to Jesus. They came. And they believed too.

It all started with a simple question. It all started with an act of love.

When the rich young ruler came to Jesus and asked what he must do to inherit eternal life, Jesus listed some of the "easiest" of the Ten Commandments. The rich young ruler was confident he had never murdered anyone, committed adultery, stolen, defrauded, or given false testimony and that he had honored his father and mother. You can almost see his chest puff up with pride as he declared to Jesus, "All these I have kept since I was a boy" (Mark 10:20).

But Jesus wasn't done with the list:

Jesus looked at him and loved him. "One thing you
lack," he said. "Go, sell everything you have and give
to the poor, and you will have treasure in heaven.
Then come, follow me."
MARK 10:21

Notice that Jesus "looked at him and loved him." Jesus cared for this young man. But he knew he had to shatter his pride.

Jesus gave him a heart-revealing, sin-unveiling command to go and sell it all, give the proceeds to the poor, and then come and follow him. From that moment on, the rich young ruler knew he was a sinner. He came to Jesus thinking he was good and left knowing he fell short. He had not kept the law perfectly, as he thought he had. He couldn't keep the tenth commandment, "Thou shalt not covet."

Still, I think we will see the rich young ruler in heaven. Before we can accept the grace and mercy of Jesus, we need to accept that we are sinners in need of a Savior. For the first time in his life, the rich young ruler knew he was spiritually bankrupt. It's hard for me to imagine that Jesus wouldn't, at some point after shattering his self-reliance, extend his hand of mercy to reconstruct this now spiritually desperate man from the inside out.

Loving others looks different with different people. Jesus used an intriguing declaration with Nicodemus. He asked an unexpected question with the woman who viewed herself as a sinner, and he issued a surprising command to the young ruler who thought he was a saint.

As a roofer, I grew accustomed to using different tools for different roofing jobs. When tearing off three-tab shingles, a pitchfork works best because it cuts between the nails and allows you to roll back massive segments of the old roof before discarding them. The Estwing roofing hammer splits wooden shake shingles on one side and hammers nails on the other. There's a tool for slicing asphalt shingles, a tool for making chalk lines, a tool for cutting metal, and a tool for pulling nails. All these tools—and then some—are used, depending on the job and the phase of the roofing process.

In the same way, Jesus used different "tools" at different times to demonstrate his love. With Nicodemus it was a declaration, a shocking truth that, like a screwdriver, torqued his attention to the message of Jesus. With the woman at the well it was a question that, like a pry bar, opened her heart to a spiritual conversation. With the rich young ruler Jesus used a command that, like a hammer, shattered his sense of self-righteousness.

Love was the driving force in Jesus' life, and he radically broke through the social boundaries of his day to love the lost and hurting by dining with tax collectors and sinners, healing lepers, and on and on. He knew how to demonstrate his love at the right time with the right person in the right way. Do you?

God's Spirit will show you how to love others with the opportunities available to you in that moment. After all, "the fruit of the Spirit is love" (Galatians 5:22).

LOVING BEYOND YOUR COMFORT ZONE

One Thanksgiving my ma invited my wife and me to spend the holiday with her and Janet. Janet was the elderly lady Ma took care of. She was in her late sixties and had lost many of her faculties. She picked at her face compulsively, leaving bloody scabs and scars. She also struggled to eat by herself.

I had been looking forward to hanging out with my ma and my wife on Thanksgiving—not some lady who required so much attention. But we met at a buffet restaurant named Furr's. (Hint: Never name a restaurant after something that implies there might be hair in your food.)

After selecting our food and carrying Janet's tray to a booth, we settled in with Ma and Janet on one side and my wife and me on the other.

As Janet struggled to eat, her food often dropped from her mouth onto her blouse. Ma just kept talking to us and matter-of-factly wiped it away. When Janet reached up to pick at the scabs on her face, Ma would gently redirect her, taking her twisted hand from her cheek and setting it back down on the table with a patient, "No picking, Janet."

When Janet needed something, Ma took care of it, almost intuitively knowing what she needed. She talked to Janet as if she had full use of her faculties. She included Janet in the conversation, even though Janet's mumbled responses were often nonsensical.

I was frustrated—and a little sick to my stomach. The food falling from Janet's mouth, combined with her bloody scabs, took my appetite away.

Then Ma said, "I need to use the bathroom. Excuse me for a moment."

The pity party inside my head ramped up into high gear. *Oh no! Now it will just be her and us.* As Janet sat awkwardly across the table, I averted my gaze to avoid making eye contact. Of course, my lovely and love-fueled wife was doing her best to make conversation. Janet responded with mumbled words between bites.

Then with absolutely no warning, Janet suddenly looked at us and spoke these words completely clearly: "Your mom is the only person on this planet who really loves me."

My wife and I were shocked. We couldn't believe she had spoken so clearly. And we were amazed by what she said.

Like a two-by-four to my soul's thick skull, I grasped the power of love and keenly felt how far I fell short when it came to loving someone outside my comfort zone.

Jesus was loving Janet through my ma. We are privileged to do the same with everyone we know and everyone we meet.

If you want to be radical like Jesus, you must use every tool at your disposal to love them like Jesus did with Nicodemus, the woman at the well, and the rich young ruler. Sometimes it's a statement that rivets their attention to the conversation. Sometimes it's the pry bar of a good question. Sometimes it's a hammer of hard truth. We must use the right tools of love in the right way at the right time. Like Ken and Floy did with Rosaria decades ago. Like my ma did with Janet that Thanksgiving Day.

RADICAL LIKE JESUS CHALLENGE #8
Difficulty: Hard

Grab a Christian friend and drive to a part of your city or town where there is a high concentration of people who are homeless. Ask one of them if you can buy them something to eat and, if they are willing, do it. Sit down with them as they eat and have a conversation—listen to their story.

And don't forget that sharing the Good News of Jesus is one of the best ways you can love them!

Note: If you live in an area where there is little or no homeless population, or you believe that it's too dangerous, then develop your own equivalent Radical like Jesus Challenge.

9

FOLLOW

"Come, follow me," Jesus said, "and I will send you out to fish for people."
At once they left their nets and followed him.

MATTHEW 4:19-20

On August 19, 1973, the day before my ninth birthday, *Enter the Dragon*, starring the one and only Bruce Lee, premiered in Los Angeles.

Soon the movie was released in theaters across the United States and a legend was born. Before the release of this one-of-a-kind movie, Bruce Lee was known in the United States as Kato, the high-flying, fist-throwing sidekick of the Green Hornet in the 1960s television series. He was another overlooked, underestimated Asian actor typecast by the largely white Hollywood community.

But *Enter the Dragon* hit the movie establishment like a one-inch punch to the solar plexus and catapulted Bruce Lee to the upper echelon of Hollywood fame. Sadly, he died a month before the Hollywood premiere, so he never got the satisfaction of seeing

87

the full impact of his brilliant acting and martial arts legacy as it spread around the world.

The movie, made for less than one million dollars, went on to make hundreds of millions of dollars worldwide. It ushered in a whole new genre of martial arts movies in Hollywood. Chuck Norris, Jean-Claude Van Damme, Jackie Chan, and many, many others owe much of their career success to Bruce Lee.

One of my favorite scenes in *Enter the Dragon* is when Bruce Lee takes on a continuous stream of more than fifty attackers—sadly, I counted them—using various weapons. But his final weapon in the culminating scene of the four-minute-long fight—sadly, I timed it—was the nunchaku. Today, they are often called nunchucks.

If you're not familiar with martial arts, nunchucks originated as Japanese fighting weapons. They consist of two twelve- to fourteen-inch-long pieces of rounded wood connected by a chain or rope. These two sticks are whipped in a continuous circular motion around one's body creating a sort of defensive shield against an attacker. They can also be used offensively to hit, block, or immobilize an opponent. Those skilled in nunchucks look quite intimidating as they work this classic weapon with speed and precision.

In the movie, Bruce Lee worked them so blindingly fast that his attacker stood with a look of awe on his face before being knocked out cold by these whirling sticks of destruction.

The nunchuck scene—which made up less than thirty seconds in Lee's four-minute fight—hooked me.

What's the first thing I did as a young, impressionable preteen after watching this movie for the first time? I, along with tens of thousands of other Bruce Lee wannabees from across the United States, bought nunchucks.

The problem was simple. I didn't know how to work them properly, which led to many bruises and Christian school kid curse words like "darn it," "dang it," and "son of a gun."

While *Enter the Dragon* inspired me, it was a high schooler named Rodney who trained me.

Rodney frequently hung out in our neighborhood with his best friend, Vince. Rodney could work nunchucks. He was good. Doubly impressive was the fact that he could do two at a time. He worked them so fast, you could barely see them as he spun them around. As a third-degree black belt, he was the closest thing I knew to a martial arts expert. So I asked him to help me. He wholeheartedly agreed.

Rodney positioned me in front of him. Five feet apart from each other, we stood face-to-face while holding our nunchucks—his were way cooler than mine.

"Do what I do," he said.

Starting in slow motion, he covered the basic nunchuck movements one by one. I mirrored him move for move until I had the first one down perfectly. Then Rodney added another slightly harder move.

With each sequential move, Rodney said, "Do what I do." I mirrored him until I had it down.

After each martial arts lesson, I'd spend hours in my unfinished basement room, where I had plenty of space to move, practicing the nunchuck moves I had just learned.

This went on week after week and month after month until I began to master this weapon.

Surprisingly, Rodney's training approach was closer to the form of "discipleship" described in the New Testament than most discipleship strategies today.

The Western idea of discipling focuses on information. The Eastern idea of discipling focuses on formation. To disciple is to form a student—to mold them into the image of their sensei, their master, their teacher.

That's why Jesus said to his disciples, "The student is not above the teacher, but everyone who is fully trained will be like their teacher" (Luke 6:40).

As Christians, our master is Jesus. We are to mirror his every move. As 1 John 2:6 reminds us, "Whoever claims to live in him must live as Jesus did." Being Jesus' disciples means seeking—in the power of the Holy Spirit—to live as Jesus did. Being his disciples means following him.

When we read the Gospels, we can, in a sense, hear Jesus through his Holy Spirit calling, "Do what I do."

This was how Jesus trained his disciples.

In Matthew 4:19, while walking along the Sea of Galilee, two prospective disciples, Peter and Andrew, were busy about their livelihood of fishing when they heard the call. "'Come, follow me,' Jesus said, 'and I will send you out to fish for people.'" Did they respond with "We're busy now, maybe tonight" or "Sure, let's hang out together after synagogue this weekend"?

No. As Matthew 4:20 indicates, "At once they left their nets and followed him."

Bible scholars believe this was not the first time Jesus had met Peter and Andrew. It's highly likely they were among the disciples mentioned in John 2:11 who were with Jesus at the wedding in Cana. But in Matthew 4, Jesus was officially calling them to follow him. Being a disciple of Jesus required them to follow and to fish.

FOLLOWING CLOSELY

"Come, follow me" (Matthew 4:19).

This brand of following was literal (to go where he went), actual (to do what he did), and nuanced (to do what he did in the way that he did it). In their excellent book *Sitting at the Feet of Rabbi Jesus: How the Jewishness of Jesus Can Transform Your Faith*,

Ann Spangler and Lois Tverberg describe what following a rabbi in ancient Jewish culture looked like:

> To follow a rabbi meant something other than sitting in a classroom and absorbing his lectures. Rather, it involved a literal kind of following, in which disciples often traveled with, lived with, and imitated their rabbis, learning not only from what they said but from what they did—from their reactions to everyday life as well as from the manner in which they lived. The task of the disciple was to become as much like the rabbi as possible.[1]

Like an apprentice following his boss or a kung fu student following her sensei, the disciples followed Jesus. How do we know this? Here are just a few instances that show how the disciples, filled with the power of the Holy Spirit after Jesus ascended into heaven, followed his example:

- Jesus was so passionate about God's honor, he cleansed the Temple (see John 2:13-22). The disciples became so passionate about God's honor, they cleansed the church of Ananias and Sapphira (see Acts 5:1-11).
- Jesus was so compassionate, he touched and healed a leper (see Mark 1:40-45). The disciples were so compassionate, they touched and healed a man who could not walk (see Acts 3:6-10).
- Jesus was so bold, he stood up against the religious rulers and confronted them (see Matthew 23:1-33). The disciples were so bold that they stood up against these same religious leaders and disobeyed their command to keep quiet about Jesus (see Acts 5:40-42).

The disciples followed Jesus and in the process became like him. Even the Sanhedrin, the same Jewish rulers who plotted Jesus' death on the cross, noticed: "When they saw the courage of Peter and John and realized that they were unschooled, ordinary men, they were astonished and they took note that these men had been with Jesus" (Acts 4:13).

The disciples copied the moves of their Messiah, and it was obvious to everyone around them.

Never stop pursuing Jesus. Never stop following your sensei. Think of him, learn from him, and imitate him—until you are fully like him.

As you do, you'll learn to fish.

CATCHING PEOPLE, NOT FISH

Following Jesus, being his disciple, is inextricably linked to evangelism. "I will send you out to fish for people," Jesus said in Matthew 4:19. Jesus was equating evangelism to fishing.

If you truly follow Jesus, you are going to follow him to the fishing hole.

Dr. Dann Spader, founder of Sonlife, often talks about Jesus and the many "fishing trips" he took his disciples on. He showed them what it looked like to live a life on mission. They watched him not only cast out a legion of demons from a tormented man but also send him back to his community on mission to declare what Jesus had done for him (see Luke 8:26-39). Jesus caught this lost man's soul and then turned him into a fisherman.

Four of the disciples—Peter, Andrew, James, and John—were very familiar with fishing for fish. But Jesus, over the course of three and a half years, showed them how to fish for people.

The closest thing I had to a father figure growing up was my grandpa. He was a quiet man with a big barrel chest and large, powerful arms. His giant, Hulk-like hands were so big that he couldn't find a wedding ring big enough to fit his sausage-sized fingers. His dark hair and olive skin made him look like an old-school mafia guy, even though he came from a long line of coal miners from Wales.

Every summer Grandpa and Grandma took me on a two-week camping and fishing trip deep in the majestic mountains of Colorado. My family lived in a high-crime area of Denver, so I eagerly anticipated these annual escapes from the fistfights and sirens.[2]

But what I looked forward to most was not gazing at the beauty of the Rocky Mountains at sunrise or even looking at the Milky Way splashed across the blanket of black sky, far from city lights. No, as much as I loved these things, what I loved most was spending hours on end with Grandpa on the bank of a river or the shore of a lake.

Actually, I didn't enjoy fishing all that much—what a lot of work for a little result! Rainbow trout that live above 10,000 feet are quite small compared to their flatland cousins. It wasn't fishing that I loved. It was being with Grandpa.

My grandfather was a master fisherman. When he taught me to fish, he said, "Do what I do." And I did.

Grandpa baited his hook; I baited mine. He switched from worms to salmon eggs; I switched too. He put on a lure; I put the exact same kind on my line. When he cast toward a certain spot, I went for that same hole, trying my best not to tangle our lines.

Down deep inside I had two motivations. First, I wanted to catch fish. If I was going to spend a day in the hot sun, I might as well catch my limit. But second and more important, I wanted my grandpa to be proud of me.

And he was. Whether or not I caught any fish, he was proud I was with him, imitating his every move.

What's true of Grandpa is true of Jesus. If we want to effectively fish for people, we must imitate what we see him doing in the Gospels.

But sometimes we need others to show us how.

MASTER FISHERMAN, EVANGELISM SENSEI, AND PERSONAL MENTOR

When I think of someone in my life who is following Jesus wholeheartedly and fishing for people effectively, I think of my friend and mentor Dave Gibson.

Dave is a force of nature. He is tall and has a deep voice. When he speaks, you think of the voice of God speaking to Charlton Heston's Moses from the burning bush or James Earl Jones reading Scripture. But it's more than his deep voice; it's his deep commitment to Jesus and the Scriptures. He sprinkles his sentences with Bible verses and peppers his prayers with passages. Dave speaks of Jesus as his best friend, Redeemer, and King.

Dave is one of the most respected and well-connected leaders in the world of missions and evangelism I have ever met. Why? Because he is relentlessly faithful at fishing for people.

Dave's goal is one-a-day gospel conversations. That's what he prays for. That's what he looks for. And, usually, God answers his prayer.

I talk to Dave on the phone several times a week, and he usually has another story of someone he shared Jesus with that day. Of course, not everyone puts their faith in Jesus on the spot, but they have a chance to, because Dave is committed to sharing the gospel and inviting them to respond.

That's why Dave is so respected. He lives it. He breathes it. He is a fisher of men.

I saw Dave in action firsthand at a restaurant in Scottsdale, Arizona. A young server named Sandra approached us to take our order. Dave immediately engaged her in a conversation, smiling like a kind grandfather and asking her how she was doing. His disarming and engaging personality immediately set her at ease. Then he put me on the spot. "Sandra," Dave said, turning toward me, "my friend Greg here has a great app that he and his team developed called Life in 6 Words. He'd love to show it to you if you have a minute."

She smiled and nodded.

Dave is notorious not only for sharing the gospel with others but also for putting his fellow believers in the evangelism hot seat.

I took out my phone, opened my Life in 6 Words app, and asked her how she would describe her life in six words. With the push of a button, fourteen words populated the screen for her to choose from. She studied the words: Relationships, Freedom, Fun, God, Meaningless, Happiness, Family, Struggles, Adventure, Money, Purpose, Routine, Broken, and Pain.

Then something broke in her. Tears filled her eyes. "Excuse me for just a moment," she said as she left our table.

Dave and I looked at each other. "One of those words triggered something inside her," Dave whispered.

He was right. Minutes later Sandra returned, composed and willing to talk. She explained how the words in the app had brought her physical and relational struggles to the surface. Then she opened her soul to us.

Dave, responding as a compassionate counselor and pastor, put her at ease. Lifting my phone, I asked if I could show her the six words of the gospel message.

The restaurant was busy, but she was fully locked in on the conversation. She wanted to see the six words.

I swiped to the part of the app displaying the six words of the GOSPEL acrostic, along with a brief sentence explaining each word.

GOD created us to be with him.
OUR sins separate us from God.
SINS cannot be removed by good deeds.
PAYING the price for sin, Jesus died and rose again.
EVERYONE who trusts in him alone has eternal life.
LIFE with Jesus starts now and lasts forever.

As I swiped through each screen of the GOSPEL, Dave and I took turns sharing. When we got to the final screen that asked if she was ready to put her faith in Jesus, Sandra said yes. In the middle of the busy, noisy restaurant, she took the first step in her walk with Jesus.

Six months later, Dave and I went back to the restaurant. We asked our server if we could speak to Sandra, but it was her day off. So we jumped in and opened a gospel conversation with our new server. When we asked if we could show her the Life in 6 Words app, she said, "Oh, Sandra already took me through that app."

Sandra was already actively sharing the gospel! We learned later that she was plugged into a church and growing in her faith. She had heard Jesus' call to move beyond simply putting her faith in Christ. She was following him.

Stories like this are not uncommon for Dave Gibson. Why? Because he has embraced the call and the cause of Christ.

Dave Gibson is my Bruce Lee of relational evangelism. He is my sensei. He is the master fisherman who I copy move for move. He is the one person in my life who can say, "Do what I do," and I do it, just like the apostle Paul said to the Corinthians: "Follow my example, as I follow the example of Christ" (1 Corinthians 11:1).

Find your own version of a Dave Gibson who has forsaken everything else to follow Jesus and fish for people.

When you do, you'll catch a lot of fish!

RADICAL LIKE JESUS CHALLENGE #9
Difficulty: Medium

Begin to pray about finding one person you can follow as they follow Christ. Look for someone who is actively sharing Jesus who you can begin to build a deeper relationship with. Once you identify someone who would be a good spiritual mentor, prayerfully approach them and ask if they would be willing to disciple you. In the meantime, download the free Life in 6 Words app, get familiar with it, and start using it to "fish for people."

Bonus: If you're up to it, buy some nunchucks.

10

PRAY

Jesus often withdrew to lonely places and prayed.

LUKE 5:16

I'LL NEVER FORGET THE DAY—APRIL 20, 1999.

It was a beautiful spring morning in Colorado. The warm sunshine and chirping birds made it feel like all was well with the world. It was a perfect day to gather a handful of youth leaders and encourage them to register for our upcoming Dare 2 Share conference in Denver.

That year's event theme was "When all hell breaks loose . . . strike back." The tour, based on Ephesians 6:10-20, was designed to equip teenagers for spiritual warfare and evangelism.

Around 11:45 a.m., just minutes before we were going to break, the pastor of the Presbyterian church where we were meeting interrupted our gathering and said nervously, "You all may want to stop and pray. From the news reports it sounds like all hell has broken loose at Columbine High School."

Until that moment, we had no idea a shocking tragedy was unfolding in this middle-class public high school in Littleton, Colorado, fifteen miles down the road. This massacre would become the terrible yardstick by which future school shootings would be measured for years to come.

Soon riveted to the breaking news, we watched in horror as SWAT teams surrounded Columbine High School and hundreds of teenagers rushed out with trembling hands raised in the air. Bloodied teenagers burst through broken windows into the outstretched arms of police officers and paramedics. Parents frantically waited nearby, desperate to learn whether their kids had made it out alive.

Hours later, we learned the full extent of the tragedy. Two disillusioned, hate-fueled high school boys had marched into Columbine armed for battle. These two shooters methodically slaughtered twelve students and one teacher. After failing to explode the bombs they had smuggled into the school cafeteria, they headed to the library, where they systematically moved from table to table, heartlessly murdering students hiding underneath the flimsy particle board tables. Outraged at their failure to kill the hundreds of teenagers they had planned to, the murderers left behind thirteen dead and twenty-four injured before turning their guns on themselves.

All hell had broken loose at Columbine High School that day. And, tragically, this cold-blooded massacre ushered in a new era of school shootings that continues to ravage the United States.

April 20, 1999, became a turning point for me. Up until that time, Dare 2 Share was a ministry I was doing on the side. As a church planter and pastor since 1989, I was busy preaching at the growing, thriving church I loved. But Dare 2 Share was also growing. In the ministry's early days, we focused on training scores of teenagers to share their faith up and down the front range of Colorado. Now, ten years later, we were training thousands of students across the nation. Being young, naive, and a bit arrogant, I thought that I could lead both ministries for the rest of my life.

But the Columbine High School massacre was my personal wake-up call. God used it to show me the imminent danger teenagers were facing both physically as a result of school shootings, drugs, and suicide and spiritually as a result of Satan's invisible, insidious attack on their souls.

Within three months I resigned from the church to lead Dare 2 Share full time. It was time to strike back against Satan.

But how would we do that?

The answer was simple. The answer was prayer.

The only one who could change the trajectory of violence and sin was God. He was the one we would call on to turn the tide.

Since the Columbine school shooting, God has increasingly revealed to me the power and priority of prayer, both in my personal life and in my public ministry.

After all, prayer was clearly the priority for Jesus. As Luke 5:16 reminds us, "Jesus often withdrew to lonely places and prayed."

Jesus was always escaping to pray. Sometimes he even left fruitful ministry opportunities to commune with his heavenly Father (see Mark 1:35-37). Jesus understood that the most important priority was prayer.

The disciples couldn't help but see and sense this too. They heard him pray. They watched him slip away to pray on countless occasions. In Luke 11:1-4 a curious disciple asked him about it.

One day Jesus was praying in a certain place. When he finished, one of his disciples said to him, "Lord, teach us to pray, just as John taught his disciples."

He said to them, "When you pray, say:

"'Father,
hallowed be your name,
your kingdom come.
Give us each day our daily bread.
Forgive us our sins,
	for we also forgive everyone who sins against us.
And lead us not into temptation.'"

This prayer has been nicknamed "The Lord's Prayer," but as someone once said, it's really "The Believer's Prayer." It is the model Jesus gave us for talking to our heavenly Father. This short prayer packs a big punch and provides every Christ follower with a simple outline for how to pray like Jesus did.

An easy-to-remember PRAY acrostic captures this outline:

Praise: "Father, hallowed be your name."
Request: "Your kingdom come. Give us each day our daily bread."
Admit: "Forgive us our sins, for we also forgive everyone who sins against us."
Yield: "And lead us not into temptation."

This simple outline can have a massive impact on the way you pray. Let's explore each of these segments more deeply and more personally.

PRAISE

Spending time in praise and worship of God is crucial. There's intimacy in calling him "Father," which implies love and relationship.

Yet paradoxically the phrase Jesus attached to the Father—"hallowed be your name"—also implies awe and worship, for his name is to be set apart above every other name.

Exodus 3 recounts God speaking to Moses from the burning bush and sending him to Pharaoh to bring the Israelites out from Egyptian bondage. As Moses tries to negotiate his way out of God's call, he asks God,

> "Suppose I go to the Israelites and say to them,
> 'The God of your fathers has sent me to you,' and
> they ask me, 'What is his name?' Then what shall I
> tell them?"
>   God said to Moses, "I AM WHO I AM. This is what
> you are to say to the Israelites: 'I AM has sent me to you.'"
> EXODUS 3:13-14

Your Father God is the great I AM, the eternally self-existent one, the one who spoke the universe into creation by the word of his power and holds it together by the strength of his might (see Isaiah 45:18). He is holy, just, righteous, loving, merciful, gracious, and so much more. He deserves your worship and praise.

But at the same time, he is your dad. You can call him "Father" and approach him with holy boldness through the shed blood and torn body of the Lord Jesus Christ (see Ephesians 3:12).

If this doesn't cause you to break out in song, nothing will.

Learn to love praising him for his intimacy ("Father") and for his majesty ("hallowed be your name").

Stop and spend a few minutes praising him for who he is right now. If you need a kickstart, open almost anywhere in the Psalms and read a chapter or two out loud to God.

Effective, Jesus-like prayer starts with praise.

REQUEST

There are two requests here. The first is for God's agenda to unfold ("your kingdom come") and the second is for the provision of our needs ("Give us each day our daily bread").

We often jump into prayer and rattle off a list of requests that would make Santa Claus blush. Far too many times we treat the Father like a genie and prayer like the bottle we rub.

Don't get me wrong, your prayer requests are gladly received by the Father. He actually wants to answer your prayers. Jesus put it this way in Matthew 7:7-11:

> Ask and it will be given to you; seek and you will find; knock and the door will be opened to you. For everyone who asks receives; the one who seeks finds; and to the one who knocks, the door will be opened.
>
> Which of you, if your son asks for bread, will give him a stone? Or if he asks for a fish, will give him a snake? If you, then, though you are evil, know how to give good gifts to your children, how much more will your Father in heaven give good gifts to those who ask him!

But perhaps before you give him your requests for the "daily bread" of financial provision, health, and such, it would be appropriate to pray for his Kingdom to come. After all, his Kingdom agenda trumps your earthly one.

Praying for God's Kingdom to come includes praying for revival and awakening to sweep your continent, country, and community. Central to this Kingdom focus is intercession that prays for the lost to be saved (see Romans 10:1) and the saved to be sent (see Matthew 9:38). How much time did Jesus spend weeping over the lost souls around him, asking the Father to save them? How much time did he spend weeping over the clueless believers around him, asking God to send them out into the fields that were ripe for harvest? How much time are you spending in intercessory prayer for the lost to be saved and the saved to be sent?

Spend a few minutes right now asking God to work in the heart of someone in your life who doesn't yet know Jesus as their Savior. Ask God to convict them of sin and of their need for a Savior. Then dare to ask him to give you an opportunity to share the gospel with that person soon, even today. Intercede for them.

Then ask for your "daily bread."

ADMIT

Before we came to faith in Jesus, God was like a judge, and we were like condemned criminals. But once we put our trust in Christ, based on his finished work on the cross, we were adopted into that judge's family and became his beloved children. We are no longer under condemnation (see Romans 8:1). Instead, we are coheirs with Christ (see Romans 8:17).

We no longer need God's forgiveness as a judge, because we are once and for all forgiven (see Colossians 2:13-14). But we do need forgiveness from our heavenly Father when we, as children, disobey him. This forgiveness has nothing to do with our eternal salvation but everything to do with our daily sanctification.

First John 1:9 puts it this way: "If we confess our sins, he is faithful and just and will forgive us our sins and purify us from all unrighteousness." So admit your sins to God (hint: he knows them anyway.) Confess the sins you remember, and he will purify you from the ones you don't as well.

This essential part of the Lord's prayer helps you keep short accounts with God and make sure that there are no "blessing blockers" between you and your divine Dad.

YIELD

You must be led by God himself, not into temptation, but into the victorious Christian life. As you yield to his Holy Spirit, you can walk in the victory that Jesus purchased for you on the cross. This victory is not just from the penalty of sin, but from its power. As Paul wrote in Galatians 5:16, "Walk by the Spirit, and you will not gratify the desires of the flesh."

Crystal Woodman Miller is a friend of mine. As a sixteen-year-old nominal Christian she typically partied with her friends on Saturday night and then headed to church on Sunday morning. She knew the dual life was wrong, but, after all, everyone was doing it.

Then came that fateful day, April 20, 1999, at Columbine High School. She heard what sounded like fireworks down the hallway when a teacher came screaming for the students to take cover. Being in the school library, she and two fellow students took cover under their table as the sound of gunshots came closer and closer. Soon the two shooters were in the room, walking from table to table and shooting student after student, based on their looks, their skin color, or their belief in God.

It was underneath that table that Crystal knew she was going to die, so she prayed in desperation, "God, if you save me from this, I'll serve you with all of my heart for the rest of my life." She fully yielded herself to God amid the smell of gunpowder and the sound of her fellow students' screams.

And God answered her desperate prayer. Although the library was the location where most of the victims were killed or wounded that day, as far as Crystal knows, the table under which she and two other students hid was the only one in the library untouched by gunfire. She escaped with a handful of others physically unscathed.

Twenty-five years later, Crystal is still on fire for God. Her prayer of yielding underneath that desk did its work. God has led her not into temptation but in deliverance from the evil one. She has published two books on the subject and travels the nation speaking of her ordeal and the urgency of the power of the gospel to transform young people's lives.[1]

But you don't need tragedy to unfold around you to yield yourself to God. You can kneel before the cross of Christ in the silent sanctuary of your soul and yield yourself fully to him right now.

I encourage you to do that. Get on your knees right now, wherever you are, and yield yourself fully to God. You might offer up a prayer like this: "My Father in heaven, I yield myself fully to you right now. Guide me in your path. Protect me from sin and Satan. Lead me not into temptation, but deliver me from the evil one. May I consistently walk in victory as I learn to constantly depend on your Spirit. In Jesus' name I pray, amen."

If you want to be radical like Jesus, learn to PRAY like Jesus.

RADICAL LIKE JESUS CHALLENGE #10
Difficulty: Medium

Go to a local public school (before or after hours, of course) and walk around the school four times, praying through the acrostic. The first time around, *praise* God for who he is and what he has done. The second time, *request* that God's Kingdom come to your local school and every school in your town or city through the words and witness of its Christian students, teachers, and administrators. The third time around, *admit* how you've fallen short in reaching people for Jesus in your world. And on the last time around, *yield* yourself fully to God to be used by him to reach others for Jesus.

11

SHINE

*Let your light shine before others, that they may see your good deeds
and glorify your Father in heaven.*

MATTHEW 5:16

THERE'S NOTHING QUITE AS DISORIENTING and terrifying as getting lost in the mountains at night. I speak from personal experience.

My buddy Donnie Coxsey, an experienced outdoorsman, introduced me to the wonderful world of elk hunting. He had previously taken me on several antelope-hunting expeditions across the windswept plains of Wyoming. But elk hunting with Donnie was different. To reach his favorite hunting site required a rigorous trek into the Rocky Mountains of Colorado.

Loading up his Ford F-150 truck before dawn, we set out on our adventure into the majestic mountain range, first on a highway, then on gravel roads, and finally on bumpy dirt roads. A few hours later we arrived at one of his prized hunting spots deep in the rugged Rockies. After we quickly set up camp, Donnie laid out the plan. "Go up that mountain," he said, pointing to the giant mountain southwest of the campsite. "Get toward the top and wait there, because that's where the elk usually graze." (He had been there the previous week to check out the grazing patterns of the herd in that area.)

"I'll go over there," he said, pointing to the mountain just north of my mountain. "If you get an elk, shoot two more times, and I'll make my way up your mountain and help you gut it and pack it out."

As a testament to his hunting prowess, Donnie's freezer at home was always full of wild game, so I didn't doubt his instructions. Grabbing the 300 Weatherby rifle he was loaning me, I trekked up the big mountain.

By the time I reached my perch atop the mountain, I was drenched in sweat from the climb. The perspiration, combined with the coolness of the morning air, left me shivering until the warm sun climbed higher in the crisp blue sky. The rustling of the leaves, the sounds of the birds, and the presence of the Spirit reminded me of the grandeur of the one who designed the breathtaking beauty all around me.

With my eyes peeled for antlers and fur and my ears tuned to breaking branches, I waited hour after hour for a cow elk to appear so I could, like Donnie, fill my freezer with a year's full of delicious elk meat.

Sadly, I spotted nothing bigger than a chipmunk that day.

As the sun began to drop and the air cooled, it was clearly time to get back to camp. Grabbing my backpack of half-eaten food, I slung my rifle across my back and began the trek down the mountain. But I had miscalculated how long it would take to get back.

As dusk moved to dark, my heart rate accelerated. I strained my eyes just to see a few feet in front of me. Then the realization hit me like a bullet. I was lost.

My mind raced. *Do I fire a couple of shots in the air to let Donnie know I'm okay? Do I just sit down in the middle of the forest and wait until morning? Are there bears in this area, and are they hungry for lost preachers?*

Panicked prayers catapulted from my heart to heaven. *God, please let me find my way out of here. Please keep me safe. Please get me back to camp.*

Slowly and carefully, I felt my way through the pitch-blackness of the trees. But just as I was about to give up and hunker down for a bone-chilling, far-below-freezing, potentially hypothermic night, I caught a glimpse of something flickering in the distance between the trees. Relief flooded through me. The dancing light in the distance was a campfire. I didn't know whose it was, but I knew that where there was a campfire, there was a camp.

With my eyes riveted to the dancing flames, I cautiously moved through the trees toward the glimmering light. After a quarter mile of slow, meticulous progress, I broke free from the forest. The blazing fire was now clearly visible, as was the individual standing by it—Donnie. Deducing I was lost, he had built the biggest campfire possible, hoping I would see it and make my way toward camp.

The light from the fire rescued me that night.

A BEACON OF HOPE

There's something about a light shining in the darkness that becomes a beacon of hope. Maybe that's why Jesus said, "Let your light shine before others, that they may see your good deeds and glorify your Father in heaven" (Matthew 5:16).

We live in a world that is spiritually dark. Despair and fear are frequent companions for those lost in the cold, black night. But when you shine a light in the darkness, the lost can find their way to safety when they follow your light to its ultimate source—Jesus himself.

How can you build a campfire so big and bright that it cannot be missed through the trees? Jesus gives you the secret for building this fire in the verses just before he commands you to "let your light shine before others":

Blessed are the poor in spirit
    for theirs is the kingdom of heaven.
Blessed are those who mourn,
    for they will be comforted.
Blessed are the meek,
    for they will inherit the earth.
Blessed are those who hunger and thirst for righteousness,
    for they will be filled.
Blessed are the merciful,
    for they will be shown mercy.
Blessed are the pure in heart,
    for they will see God.
Blessed are the peacemakers,
    for they will be called children of God.
Blessed are those who are persecuted because of
        righteousness,
    for theirs is the kingdom of heaven.

Blessed are you when people insult you, persecute you and falsely say all kinds of evil against you because of me. Rejoice and be glad, because great is your reward in heaven, for in the same way they persecuted the prophets who were before you.

MATTHEW 5:3-12

Donnie lit kindling with a match, fed the small flame with branches, and then piled logs on until the flames danced high and shone brightly in the darkness. In the same way, Jesus shows you how to build a bonfire with your life that shines the light of Christ for those lost in darkness.

BUILDING A BLAZING BONFIRE

In these ten verses Jesus reveals the secret for living in such a countercultural way that you can't help but shine. Some call this passage of Scripture the Beatitudes. I call it "How to Build a Blazing Bonfire of Hope in a Dizzyingly Dark World."

It starts with the spark that comes from being "poor in spirit" and mourning over your sin. When you humbly realize you are spiritually bankrupt before God and become aware of your inability to save yourself, you are ready to meekly receive the gift of life through faith alone in Christ alone.

But that's just the start to becoming a light in the darkness.

You add kindling to this fire when you hunger and thirst for righteousness, instead of for your rights and delights. You add branches to this blaze when you are merciful to those who are mean to you. Purity of heart, peacemaking, and rejoicing in the midst of persecution and mockery add more logs to your fire.

These actions, these attitudes are the anti-darkness. They are the complete opposite of how the world is wired to respond. They are a bright light in a dark world.

Jesus embodied these actions and attitudes. He could confidently declare, "I am the light of the world. Whoever follows me will never walk in darkness, but will have the light of life" (John 8:12).

When you shine the light of Christ through your life by living out the Beatitudes with an attitude of love, humility, and courage, the lost will see your light flickering through the darkness, and that firelight will guide them safely home.

When my rough-and-tumble uncle Jack was radically converted to Christ, the first thing he did was share the gospel with his buddy Thumper, an Italian bodybuilder he both worked and worked out with. Thumper invited Jack over to his house where he, his parents, and all his siblings (including my hunter friend, Donnie) listened to Jack share the gospel night after night. Over spaghetti and meatballs one night and pizza the next, Jack shared the gospel with passion, power, persuasion, and persistence. One by one, over the course of a few weeks, they crossed the line of faith.

But it wasn't just Jack's words that moved them; it was his life. Jack had been transformed by Jesus. He had spent much of his adult life in jail for violence of one kind or another. But now he was poor in spirit, mourning over his past and hungry for a future serving God. He was by no means weak, but for the first time in his life, he was displaying strength under control and extending mercy to others instead of fists. He was learning, ever so slowly, how to be a peacemaker. As for rejoicing in persecution, he didn't get much practice at that since his biceps were so big that not many dared mock him for his newfound faith.

The Coxsey family saw the campfire that Jesus had built in Jack's life and in short order made their way out of the darkness and into the warmth of God's Kingdom. Soon they, too, began to shine the light of Jesus with their lives and share his message with their lips.

For the last few decades Donnie has been working at companies that sell hunting, fishing, and camping equipment. He has led countless coworkers and customers to Christ. He exemplifies the Beatitudes in his attitudes. He lets his light shine before others. They see his good works and glorify his Father in heaven.

Are you shining the light at your job or in your school or

SHINE

neighborhood? Are you known online for being a peacemaker or a troublemaker? Do you show mercy to those who wrong you? Do you mourn over your sin? Are you poor in spirit, fully depending on Jesus to save and sanctify you? Are you characterized by meekness and strength under control or by out-of-control anger? Are you pure in heart, refusing to let porn or bitterness or gossip dominate you? When's the last time you were persecuted for sharing the gospel? Were you genuinely excited about it?

Light that kindling. Start that fire. Shine like Jesus. And pass it on.

RADICAL LIKE JESUS CHALLENGE #11
Difficulty: Hard

Sit down with your spouse or a really close Christian friend and have them rate you on each of the Beatitudes from 1 to 10 (10 being strongest). Ask them why they gave you the rating they did. Make a note for each rating you receive.

_____ Blessed are the poor in spirit, for theirs is the kingdom of heaven.

_____ Blessed are those who mourn, for they will be comforted.

_____ Blessed are the meek, for they will inherit the earth.

_____ Blessed are those who hunger and thirst for righteousness, for they will be filled.

_____ Blessed are the merciful, for they will be shown mercy.

_____ Blessed are the pure in heart, for they will see God.

_____ Blessed are the peacemakers, for they will be called children of God.

____ Blessed are those who are persecuted because of righteousness, for theirs is the kingdom of heaven.

____ Blessed are you when people insult you, persecute you and falsely say all kinds of evil against you because of me. Rejoice and be glad, because great is your reward in heaven, for in the same way they persecuted the prophets who were before you.

12

PROCLAIM

He went to Nazareth, where he had been brought up, and on the Sabbath
day he went into the synagogue, as was his custom. He stood up to read,
and the scroll of the prophet Isaiah was handed to him. Unrolling it,
he found the place where it is written: "The Spirit of the Lord is on me,
because he has anointed me to proclaim good news to the poor. He has sent
me to proclaim freedom for the prisoners and recovery of sight for the blind,
to set the oppressed free, to proclaim the year of the Lord's favor."

LUKE 4:16-19

MY WIFE, DEBBIE, recently retired after teaching fifth grade for
almost thirty years at the same public school. Over those three
decades she was a witness to her students and fellow teachers.
Although she could not stand up in front of her class and preach
the gospel verbally, she could, and often did, create settings where
her fifth graders could have spiritual conversations. She simply
provided opportunities for the Christian students in her class to
talk about their faith. She also understood that, if one of her
students asked her what she believed, she could, without fear
of being fired, proclaim the message of Jesus that transformed
her life.

One day when she was teaching her students to debate, she
paired the kids off and instructed them to choose a topic. Vicki
and Dan settled on evolution versus creation. Vicki was a strong

Christian, while Dan was a devout atheist. Both fifth graders were articulate and passionate about their beliefs. Debbie anticipated she was about to witness something extraordinary.

When Vicki and Dan's time to debate in front of the class came, Dan unleashed all his arguments for evolution and against creation. For a fifth grader, he did a masterful job. But then it was Vicki's turn. She laid out the arguments for creation, and for even greater effect, she used it as an opportunity to share the gospel message.

Vicki and her family attended the church I had coplanted and copastored. She knew how to clearly share the gospel because equipping the people of Grace Church to share their faith was a core value of our church. We used the GOSPEL acrostic I'd developed to help both our students and our adults master the message of the gospel. Vicki had memorized the GOSPEL acrostic.

So after making her argument for creationism and against evolution, Vicki proclaimed, "Something even more important than believing in creation is believing in the Creator and the gospel message . . .

GOD created us to be with him.
OUR sins separate us from God.
SINS cannot be removed by good deeds.
PAYING the price for sin, Jesus died and rose again.
EVERYONE who trusts in him alone has eternal life.
LIFE with Jesus starts now and lasts forever."[1]

Vicki closed her debate with this simple explanation of the gospel message. The students, including Dan, immediately began making fun of her. Shaken to the core, Vicki asked my wife if she could step into the hallway to collect herself for a few minutes.

Sensing she was devastated by the mockery from her fellow class-mates, Debbie smiled at Vicki and nodded her approval.

Debbie rebuked the class for their cruelty and continued with the next debate. After a few minutes, she went into the hallway to check on Vicki.

Amazingly, Vicki was down on her knees with her Bible open on the floor before her. Tears were streaming down her cheeks as she prayed out loud for her classmates' salvation. She hadn't been crying because her feelings were hurt. She was crying for the souls of her classmates. She was begging God to save them from the penalty of sin and the flames of hell.

My wife's eyes filled with tears as she realized what was happening. This fifth-grade girl was more than a debater; she was a proclaimer—a bold witness for the gospel and a strong intercessor for her lost friends.

Vicki grew up and married Nick, a young man raised in our church. Now they are missionaries in Thailand, raising their six kids and teaching them how to lovingly, boldly, and wisely proclaim the GOSPEL to their friends in a country that is generally antagonistic to the gospel message.

BE BRAVE DESPITE ANTAGONISM

Imagine what it must have been like for Jesus when he returned to his hometown of Nazareth after the initial launch of his public ministry. During the months he had been away, a lot had happened. Following his baptism by John the Baptist and commissioning by the Father, he had spent forty days in the wilderness, fasting, praying, most likely planning, and most definitely fighting the temptations of the devil. He had shared the Good News of the gospel with both Nicodemus and the Samaritan woman, as well as with her entire village. He had performed two significant miracles—turning water into wine at the wedding of Cana and healing the royal official's son in Capernaum.

Now Jesus was back in the community where he had grown up and had most likely taken over the family carpentry business and become the town handyman. Having just hit his ministry stride, he came back to his hometown to make a catalytic declaration. In the small synagogue where he had attended a thousand Sabbath services, he unrolled the scroll of Scripture and read from the prophet Isaiah. "The Spirit of the Lord is on me, because he has anointed me to proclaim good news to the poor," Jesus declared. "He has sent me to proclaim freedom for the prisoners and recovery of sight for the blind, to set the oppressed free, to proclaim the year of the Lord's favor" (Luke 4:18-19).

I imagine there was an audible gasp from the crowd after what he did and said next: "Then he rolled up the scroll, gave it back to the attendant and sat down. The eyes of everyone in the synagogue were fastened on him. He began by saying to them, 'Today this scripture is fulfilled in your hearing'" (Luke 4:20-21).

This was the most powerful synagogue moment in the history of the world. Why? Because Jesus declared himself the fulfillment of the prophet's prediction in Isaiah 61:1-2. With eight simple words he proclaimed himself to be the Messiah, the fulfillment of Isaiah's prophecy seven centuries earlier.

Although his declaration was received with initial excitement (see Luke 4:22), in short order, the fickle crowd turned angry at his bold assertion and dragged him to a nearby cliff to throw him to his death.

But through God's miraculous intervention, Jesus turned around and walked right through the angry crowd, parted by God like the Red Sea before Moses (see Luke 4:29-30). His time to die had not yet come.

START WITH THOSE WHO KNOW THEY HAVE A SPIRITUAL NEED

The declaration of Jesus in the synagogue of Nazareth was powerful on two levels. First, it was a clear declaration of the Messiahship of Jesus. There was no doubt in the minds of his listeners back then (or to serious readers of Scripture today) that Jesus was claiming to be the Old Testament fulfillment to the hundreds of prophecies about a coming Messiah. To those naysayers who paint a picture of Jesus as, at best, just a good teacher, these verses become a brick wall in the middle of their heresy highway.

Second, not only were Jesus' words a clear proclamation of his identity, but they were also a clear declaration of his strategy. Jesus was sharing his ministry plan of proclaiming the Good News to those who were in bad situations financially, spiritually, physically, and socially.

Jesus' plan involved targeting the lowest of the low with his message of hope. He was going to the poor, the prisoners, the blind, and the oppressed. His plan wasn't just to be nice to the downtrodden. His plan was super strategic.

Why? Because the poor, marginalized, and hurting tend to be far more open to the gospel than the rich, popular, and powerful!

This is a strategy many Christians have missed out on when it comes to evangelism. We must, like Jesus, seek first to reach those who are hurting.

Charles Spurgeon, "the Prince of Preachers," built a church in London in the nineteenth century that was often packed with the poor. In his classic sermon "Preaching for the Poor," he gives a simple explanation of why reaching the poor is strategic:

> It is one delightful mark of Christ's dispensation, that he aims first at the poor. "The poor have the gospel preached to them." It was wise in him to do so. If we would fire

a building, it is best to light it at the basement; so our Saviour, when he would save a world, and convert men of all classes, and all ranks, begins at the lowest rank, that the fire may burn upwards, knowing right well that what was received by the poor, will ultimately by his grace be received by the rich also.[2]

I often tell pastors and church leaders, if you want to reach a city for Christ, start with the public schools, the apartment complexes, and the trailer courts, because the young and the poor are the ones often looking and longing for hope.

Think about it. It's not usually rich people who buy lotto tickets. It's generally the poor—the ones who can least afford to spend their money gambling—who scratch lotto tickets. Why? They are looking for a way out of their trap. They are scratching for hope.

Maybe when Jesus said, "Blessed are the poor in spirit," he actually meant the poor (see Luke 6:20). Perhaps he knew that the converted poor would proclaim the Good News to their family, friends, and coworkers faster than the rich would.

This bears out in early church history. According to Walter Oetting, former professor of church history at Concordia Seminary, "The pagan Celsus scoffed at the workers in wool and leather, the rustic and ignorant persons who spread Christianity. The work was not done by people who called themselves missionaries but by rank-and-file members."[3]

In Luke 4:17-21 Jesus proclaims that the Spirit of the Lord sends him first to the poor, the prisoners, the blind, and oppressed. The great apostle Paul added an exclamation point to this in 1 Corinthians 1:26-29:

Brothers and sisters, think of what you were when you were called. Not many of you were wise by human standards;

not many were influential; not many were of noble birth. But God chose the foolish things of the world to shame the wise; God chose the weak things of the world to shame the strong. God chose the lowly things of this world and the despised things—and the things that are not—to nullify the things that are, so that no one may boast before him.

Of course, people of all classes, including the rich, can be saved and used by God. I know some very wealthy people who are rich in faith and generous to others. But by Jesus' own admission, "it is easier for a camel to go through the eye of a needle than for someone who is rich to enter the kingdom of God" (Matthew 19:24). While reaching and mobilizing the rich is possible, it is far more strategic to start by reaching and mobilizing the poor.

Not only has this been demonstrated in church history, it has also been proven by my family history.

My ma raised me and my brother on her own without alimony or government support in a very tough, very poor part of our city. TV dinners, apartment complexes, and trailer courts were our lot in life. And speaking of lots, my ma bought a lot of lotto tickets, trying to scratch us out of this lifestyle by the luck of the draw.

Ma had tried to find satisfaction in man after man, but she couldn't. Like the woman at the well, she was seeking to quench her thirst through relationships. But none would satisfy.

As a preteen, I was taught how to share the gospel, and the first person I sought to reach was my ma.

Ma was poor—poor financially and poor in spirit. But she was rich in shame.

Every time I shared the gospel, she would shoot me down with statements like "You don't know the things I've done wrong" or "I'm too big a sinner for God to save." She never thought God could forgive her, especially for the sin of almost aborting me.

But God called me to preach good news to my poor ma, to proclaim freedom from her prison of guilt, to see her healed of spiritual blindness, and to do my part in setting her free from the invisible oppression that plagued her.

Finally, after about three years of sharing the gospel with my ma, she trusted in Jesus as her Savior at our kitchen table (while smoking a cigarette)!

Watching my ma become free from the shackles of shame that had kept her bound was one of the best days of my life.

But it didn't stop with my ma. I have never stopped proclaiming this message to the rich and poor and everyone in between. Why? Because I have been anointed and appointed to go preach the gospel to the poor . . . and so have you!

Who is that poor-in-spirit person in your life who desperately needs to hear the gospel? Who do you know who needs freeing from their prison?

Jesus came to preach the gospel, and he calls us to do the same. Start today!

RADICAL LIKE JESUS CHALLENGE #12
Difficulty: Hard

Memorize the GOSPEL acrostic on page 118 word for word. Once you can articulate it without looking, practice explaining it in the mirror. Then go to dare2share.org/resources/how-to-share-the-gospel and learn how to share the gospel naturally in conversation. Then try to have a gospel conversation with one person God is putting on your heart (take them out to coffee, invite them to dinner, write them a letter, etc.). Start praying God would give you regular opportunities to share the gospel with those in your world.

13

HEAL

Jesus went through all the towns and villages, teaching in their synagogues,
proclaiming the good news of the kingdom and healing every disease
and sickness. When he saw the crowds, he had compassion on them,
because they were harassed and helpless, like sheep without a shepherd.

MATTHEW 9:35-36

THE WORD *HEALER* in conjunction with a religious leader conjures up images—not all of them good. You can't help but think of the televangelist, slap-you-on-the-forehead, name-it-claim-it shysters who seem to own the further-down-the-line cable stations.

Does that mean healings aren't real? That God doesn't heal today?

Nope.

Jesus has always been in the healing business. We see it in his earthly ministry. But we also see it today.

I saw it big time a couple decades ago.

As a young leader in youth ministry, I was invited to attend what was called "The Youth Ministry Executive Council" in Washington, DC. This was indeed a privilege. To be hobnobbing with key parachurch leaders and national denominational youth leaders for three days in our nation's capital was humbling and exciting.

At a multimillion-dollar retreat center just outside of DC, we heard experts speak on reaching young people and strategized together how to best leverage the collective strengths of our ministries for the cause of Christ. We also spent time praying together.

And it was at the designated prayer time when things got turned sideways for me.

We were instructed to gather around tables to pray together for each other and for the youth of our nation. Somehow, I found myself sitting at the Pentecostal table. Now, I love Pentecostals. Anyone who hoots and hollers at my sermon points gets a hearty amen from me. I love them, but at the time, I wasn't used to them.

Saved in a Baptist church, raised in an Independent Fundamentalist church, and the former pastor of a Plymouth Brethren church, I was familiar with the "steak" of sound doctrine but was kind of freaked out by the "sizzle" of the Holy Spirit.

The Pentecostals brought the "sizzle" to my round table's prayers that night. And it was all led by Bob.

Bob had perfect televangelist hair and a snappy, dapper suit. In a room full of youth ministry leaders, he stood out as unique . . . and way better dressed than most of us.

Bob was bigger than life. He was loud and funny and had a flair that drew people in (and freaked some people—like me—out).

As we sat, I quickly suspected that I had chosen the wrong table. Bob, like a carnival barker, asked the young leader next to him in a voice so loud that all the room could hear, "What's your prayer request, young man?" That young leader, full of the Spirit himself, said, "I want to claim a million souls for my ministry this year."

"Well, let's claim it! Let's claim it in the name of Jesus!" Bob bellowed.

And then he dove into a no-holds-barred prayer that brought heaven down and made the devil run in the opposite direction.

The "amens" and "yes, Lords" reverberated around our table like an echo chamber.

As Bob moved from person to person around the table, the prayers got louder and louder. I even threw in a "make it so, Lord" just to keep up with the automatic, charismatic, super-dramatic prayers. One after another Bob prayed for each leader's prayer request as he worked his way closer to me.

All the other tables in the room were relatively quiet. Occasionally, you could hear an "amen" from the Baptist table, but most were listening to Bob call heaven down.

Finally, my turn came. Since most of the guys at our table had asked for prayer for the expansion of their ministries, it had turned into a faith frenzy of prayer proclamations. To be honest, being the conservative at the table, I was embarrassed.

So when Bob turned to me after another full-throttle prayer and eagerly asked, "What's your prayer request, son?" I thought, *Maybe if I pray for something personal, it will calm him down a bit.*

Without thinking it through, I blurted, "My wife and I have been married for ten years and still can't have kids. We've been to the doctor, and it seems like the problem lies with me and my, well, count."

That was the wrong thing to say to Bob. He got this wild look in his eye and said, "I've prayed for hundreds of couples, and they've never failed to have kids! Gather round, boys!"

With that they all got out of their chairs and surrounded me. I was thinking, *Oh no! What have I done?* After they all placed their hands on my head (thank the Lord), Bob started his prayer, "DEAR GOD, IN THE NAME OF JESUS, I PRAY THAT YOU TOUCH THIS MAN'S SPERM AND BRING THEM TO LIFE!"

Have you ever been so embarrassed you can feel your ears turn bright red with blushing blood? But Bob wasn't done. He continued, "AND TOUCH HIS WIFE'S EGGS! AND BRING THEM TOGETHER IN A HOLY COLLISION OF LIFE AND LOVE!"

Bob prayed for what seemed like hours (it was probably less than two minutes). When he finished, he looked at me with bulging eyes and declared, "IT IS DONE! IT IS DONE IN THE NAME OF JESUS!"

It ain't done yet, Bob! I thought. *Faith without works is dead! And I don't think you can use the word "sperm" in a prayer!*

Three weeks later my wife got pregnant. As soon as we discovered it, I sent Bob a note that read, "IT IS DONE! My wife is pregnant!"

Now Bob and I may differ on some of the finer points of the Holy Spirit, healing, and prayer, but the bottom line is that Bob prayed like Jesus was standing right there. He prayed in faith, and God—thank God—heard his prayer of faith.

I was healed as a result.

Today my wife and I have two kids—Jeremy, 23, and Kailey, 19. I jokingly call Kailey "the second blessing."

Does God heal today? The answer is a resounding yes! Does he always heal? The answer is a resounding no!

When you read the Gospels, it seems like Jesus healed everyone who truly wanted to be healed. But his healings often went far beyond the physical. He healed people on every level, especially spiritually.

When Jesus saw the paralytic man in Mark 2:5, he declared, "Son, your sins are forgiven." Looking beyond the man's paralyzed body, Jesus saw his paralyzed soul and set him free because of his faith. After all, the man had consented to be dropped through a hole in the roof his friends had dug to get him in front of Jesus. They clearly had faith in Jesus.

In Matthew 9:35-38, Jesus' healing ministry was much broader than just physical healing. Yes, he was concerned about broken bodies, blind eyes, and deaf ears. But he was especially concerned about broken lives, shattered hopes, spiritually blind eyes, and spiritually deaf ears.

We can be radical like Jesus if we do what Jesus did when it comes to those who need healing around us. What did Jesus do? He saw. He felt. He imagined. He acted.

JESUS SAW

I wear contact lenses. I remember when I had to put them in for the very first time. It was a hard adjustment. It took me forty-five minutes per eye to get them in! But as hard as the adjustment was, it was completely necessary. And once I got used to them, I could never go back.

Why? Because they help me see things the way they really are. Being nearsighted, anything beyond a few feet from my face looks fuzzy. But once the contacts are in, I see things as they really are.

We need some Jesus-brand spiritual contact lenses. When Jesus "saw the crowds" in Matthew 9:36, he saw them as they really were. He saw behind the smiling facades. He saw their hurts. He saw their pain. He saw the true condition of their souls.

As someone who travels frequently for my ministry work, I spend a lot of time in airports. As I ride the moving sidewalks in terminals across the nation, I see people. My prayer is that God will help me see them through the spiritual contact lenses of Christ himself.

Healing people starts with seeing people as they really are.

JESUS FELT

Matthew continues with his description: "When he saw the crowds, he had compassion on them" (9:36).

Our word *compassion* comes from the Latin word *compassio*, which means "to suffer with," but the Greek word Matthew uses, *splagchnizomai*, is a super strong word for pity. It describes the compassion that moves someone to their core, in the very depths of their being. It describes a visceral feeling of pain in your gut, in your very bowels.

It's a gut punch. It's empathy on steroids. It's hurting down deep inside for those who hurt down deep inside.

Years ago, I was on a preaching tour in India where I preached fifty-six times in eighteen days. One day when the driver was shuttling me off to the next place, I heard a slight tap on the car window. I looked over. And then I looked down. A little girl with the saddest face I'd ever seen was pointing to her stomach and then pointing to her mouth. She did it again, over and over again, and I broke down in tears. I felt her pain in that moment. Quickly rolling down the window to beat the stoplight, I gathered what rupees I had in my pocket and dropped them into her little outstretched hands.

It was a gut punch. It was *splagchnizomai*.

We must see people. We must feel for people.

JESUS IMAGINED

"When he saw the crowds, he had compassion on them, because they were harassed and helpless, like sheep without a shepherd" (Matthew 9:36).

Jesus used his imagination when he saw the crowds. He saw them like sheep without a shepherd, harassed and helpless before a snarling, charging enemy.

Matthew uses two very descriptive Greek words for "harassed and helpless" in this passage: *skullo* and *rhipto*. *Skullo* means skinned, flayed, or lacerated. *Rhipto* carries the idea of being thrown down, like a body to the ground, like an anchor to the ocean floor.

These two adjectives convey a word picture of a wild animal—a wolf, a lion, or a bear—charging in and plowing through the flock of sheep, lacerating them with sharp claws and vicious fangs as the helpless creatures are thrown to the ground. Jesus' vivid imagination painted a bloody scene in his mind as he very likely looked at the crowds with tear-filled eyes.

In the midst of your daily life, have you ever stopped and imagined the pain people around you are going through? Imagine their secret suffering and the fear and desperation that must fill their souls. Imagine them, with tear-filled eyes, as *skullo* and *rhipto*, harassed and helpless, like sheep without a shepherd. Imagine the claws and fangs of invisible enemies—Satan and his demonic hordes—as they charge through people's lives and throw them to the ground.

Then imagine these enemies dragging people away, leaving a trail of blood along the way. Imagine the hell they are dragging people through and—ultimately—to.

When you unleash your imagination like Jesus did, you will feel compassion like Jesus did.

JESUS ACTED

"Jesus went through all the towns and villages, teaching in their synagogues, proclaiming the good news of the kingdom and healing every disease and sickness" (Matthew 9:35).

Jesus didn't just see, feel, and imagine. He *acted*.

He acted by healing disease and brokenness in the towns and villages he visited. He acted by proclaiming the Good News of the Kingdom to all who would listen.

Jesus was in the business of healing body and soul.

Can you imagine having the healing power of Jesus? Today's equivalent would be like going into the hospital in your city and, room by room, from the emergency room to the cancer ward, restoring broken bodies to full health. What joy that would bring!

But guess what? There are hurting people all around you. There are people all around you who are afflicted by depression, paralyzed by sin, and broken by life. See them. Feel for them. Imagine the hopelessness of their lives. And then act.

If they are sick, pray for them. You don't have to rend the heavens like Bob did, but do come boldly before the throne on their behalf. As James 5:16 reminds us, "Pray for each other so that you may be healed. The earnest prayer of a righteous person has great power and produces wonderful results" (NLT).

If they are hungry, feed them. If they are lonely, spend time with them. If they are misunderstood, seek to understand them. Then share the gospel with them just like Jesus did with so many that he healed both physically and spiritually.

See. Feel. Imagine. Act.

RADICAL LIKE JESUS CHALLENGE #13
Difficulty: Medium

Go to a local shopping mall or busy park in your area. Sit down on a bench and watch people as they walk by. See them. Try to feel the pain they may be facing in their personal lives at that very moment. Imagine them like sheep without a shepherd. Do this for thirty minutes, then journal your thoughts. Finally, ask God to give you one specific way you can take action to help those who are hurting in your world. Then do it.

14

SERVE

Now that I, your Lord and Teacher, have washed your feet,
you also should wash one another's feet.

JOHN 13:14

COMMUNITY BAPTIST CHURCH was a typical church in a typical suburb. So I decided to do something atypical. As the part-time middle school youth leader, I issued a challenge to the students on Wednesday night.

"This Sunday night we are going to take the church van down to inner-city Denver and serve the homeless. So if you have extra blankets, bring them. If you have warm jackets lying around the house that nobody uses, bring them. If you have food in your pantries that you can spare, bring it."

On Sunday evening at 6:00 p.m., twelve middle schoolers—all girls—showed up at the church, fully loaded for generosity. We made three piles: blankets, coats, and food. After rallying for a few minutes of safety instructions, we gathered in the requisite Baptist prayer circle of power, and I asked God to help us serve the cold and hungry across the city. Then we piled into the van.

It was a cold December night, but after a few tries the church van fired up nicely. Between the defrost and the hot, chatty breath of a van full of middle school girls, the light coating of ice on the windshield quickly melted away. We were off on our twenty-five-minute drive from our safe middle-class neighborhood to the boroughs and bridges of inner-city Denver.

There was only one problem. When we got there, we couldn't find anyone who was homeless.

We drove slowly around the urban corridors and under the bridges. This was my old neighborhood, so I knew this area well, but it seemed like everyone must have been staying at the Denver Rescue Mission that night. It made sense. The night was especially cold.

Just as I was about to give up and head back home to do a devotional on unmet expectations, one of the girls let out a loud, high-pitched yell. "There's one!"

"Pull over! Pull over!" they all yelled in unison, like a van full of tiny, twitchy cheerleaders.

The man was sleeping on a sidewalk grate that must have been venting some heat from somewhere. He was obviously trying to stay warm.

I pulled over and turned off the engine, but before I could give a quick pep talk to the girls, they all catapulted out of the van. And they took all the supplies with them.

I got out of the van and carefully scanned our surroundings to make sure nobody was lurking in the shadows. Concluding that the location was safe, I walked over to join the girls. They had fully surrounded the man as he lay on the grate. The girls were silent as the man awoke, looked up, and then stood with a genuine look of fear on his face. Perhaps he thought he was about to be mugged by this group of middle school girls.

Then it happened.

The girl with all the coats stepped forward and gave him *all* the coats.

No! I thought. *Give one coat to each person, not all the coats to one!*

Then the girl with all the blankets stepped forward and gave him *all* the blankets.

And the girl with all the food stepped forward and gave him *all* the food.

The man's arms overflowed with a mountain of coats and blankets and canned food as he struggled to hold it all.

Just when I was about to intervene, he asked the girls, "Why are you doing this?"

There was silence for five seconds or so—though it felt like five minutes.

One girl finally answered with tears in her eyes, "Because we love Jesus, and we love you." With that she ran up to the man and gave him a big bear hug. All the other girls followed her lead.

The man stood there in silence under a mountain of supplies embraced by a small army of Baptist middle school girls. Tears of joy flowed like small rivers down his bright red cheeks.

It may have been the first time the man had been hugged in a long time. More than the coats, blankets, and food, this man needed love.

It was Jesus hugging him through the twenty-four adolescent arms embracing him.

When's the last time you served someone—*really* served someone—without expecting anything in return?

Jesus showed us what this kind of service looks like when he washed his disciples' feet.

NOTHING TO PROVE AND NOTHING TO LOSE

In ancient Jewish culture washing feet was the job of the household slave or servant.

Think about it. In Jesus' day, people typically traveled on foot or by donkey or horse. And there were no poop-and-scoop laws. So after walking through the dirty streets of Jerusalem, the feet of the apostles were most likely crud and mud encrusted. When they gathered in the upper room on that fateful night when Jesus would be betrayed, nobody made the first move—the move to serve. The disciples took their places around the Passover table, but still nobody headed toward the basin and the towel. They were more worried about who would be sitting at Jesus' right and left in the eternal Kingdom. Nobody made the move to do the job of the slave, even after the meal was served.

So Jesus, watching, waiting, looking, and listening, made his move:

Jesus knew that the Father had put all things under his power, and that he had come from God and was returning to God; so he got up from the meal, took off his outer clothing, and wrapped a towel around his waist. After that, he poured water into a basin and began to wash his disciples' feet, drying them with the towel that was wrapped around him.

JOHN 13:3-5

Words can't express how awkward this moment must have been for the disciples in the upper room that night.

Here was the Savior of mankind, the Messiah, the Chosen One, the King of kings and Lord of lords, wrapping a towel around his waist and filling up a basin with water. Walking toward the closest disciple, he unstrapped and removed his follower's sandals one at a time and then washed his feet, splashing the dirt and dung onto his holy hands.

The first sentence of this Bible passage leaps off the page because it gives us the reason why Jesus could serve. He "knew that the Father had put all things under his power, and that he had come from God and was returning to God; so he got up from the meal." He *willingly* washed his disciples' feet.

The premise of the passage is this: when you know who you are, whose you are, where you came from, and where you are headed, you have nothing to prove and nothing to lose by serving others.

Jesus knew who he was. He was the King-in-waiting, soon to be coronated after his ascension into heaven. He knew whose he was. He was his Father's Son. He knew where he had come from. He had descended from heaven as God made flesh. He knew where he was going. After his death, burial, and resurrection, he was ascending back into heaven as the God-man.

Although we are not Jesus, the truths of this passage apply directly to us.

KNOWING WHO YOU ARE AND WHOSE YOU ARE

As believers in Jesus, we can know who we are. Jesus "has made us to be a kingdom and priests to serve his God and Father" (Revelation 1:6).

You can know whose you are. You are your Father's son or daughter (see Hebrews 2:10).

You know where you came from. You were foreknown, predestined, and chosen before the foundation of the earth (see Romans 8:29) so that you could be knit by the hands of God in your mother's womb and fearfully and wonderfully made in his image (see Psalm 139:13-14). You were born to be born again (see Titus 3:5) as a child of God.

You know where you are going. You are going straight to heaven when you die (see 2 Corinthians 5:8) and then straight back to earth someday to rule and reign with him during his Kingdom reign (see Revelation 20:4).

You have nothing to lose and everything to win when you serve others like Jesus did.

You have nothing to prove when you do the modern-day equivalent of washing the feet of those around you. Why? Because Jesus already proved your high value. He chose you, made you, redeemed you, and destined you for greatness in his eternal Kingdom!

So how can you wash the feet of those around you?

If you work with them, get their coffee, brush the snow off their windshield, and help them with their projects.

If you live with them, wash their dishes, do their laundry, and cook their food.

If you go to school with them, help them with their homework, do something extra kind for them, and listen to their problems.

Get practical. Get tactical. See yourself as a servant to them.

Don't be afraid of getting your hands dirty . . . just like Jesus.

As a child of the King, you have nothing to prove, nothing to lose, and everything—in the eternal Kingdom, anyway—to gain.

> When he had finished washing their feet, he put on his clothes and returned to his place. "Do you understand what I have done for you?" he asked them. "You call me 'Teacher' and 'Lord,' and rightly so, for that is what I am. Now that I, your Lord and Teacher, have washed your feet, you also should wash one another's feet."
> JOHN 13:12-14

RADICAL LIKE JESUS CHALLENGE #14
Choose one of the following:

Difficulty: Hard

Go to a local rescue mission, homeless shelter, or food bank and serve for a day.

Difficulty: Medium

Do all the chores in your house (cleaning, dishes, trash, laundry, etc.) without drawing any attention to it. If someone asks why, just tell them, "Because I wanted you to know I care about you."

15

ABIDE

I am the vine, you are the branches. He who abides in Me,
and I in him, bears much fruit; for without Me you can do nothing.

JOHN 15:5, NKJV

It was a beautiful Italian summer morning in Alessandria. Lush, green vineyards stretched as far as the eye could see across the rolling hills. Brilliant sunshine washed across the towering cathedral that crested the hilltop of the nearest village. The giant bell of the ancient Catholic church marked each passing hour, reminding both the locals and the tourists that God was watching.

My young family, along with the other guests of La Rocca Vineyards Bed & Breakfast, gathered hungrily around a large wooden table stacked with Italian breakfast cuisine.

"Why do you call this place La Rocca?" I asked Tracey, the owner of the B and B. "What does it mean?"

"It means 'The Rock,'" she said with a warm smile. "We call it that for two reasons. First, this house is literally built into a rock, which gives the house stability. But second, there is an even more important reason we call it La Rocca. You see, years ago my husband abandoned me and our two children and left me to raise the kids alone. Through the years, I've learned that it is Jesus Christ who is our real and ultimate rock."

I could tell she had told this story a thousand times to a thousand guests. She used it to point to Jesus as the only rock worth building your life and family upon.

As we finished the last of the breakfast spread, Tracey asked me, "Would you and your family like to help prune the vineyard today?"

Seeing the approving smile on my wife's face, I said, "Of course we would! What would give us a more authentic Italian experience than pruning a vineyard?"

Tracey gathered the necessary tools for the morning's work. Before walking out to the vineyard, she pulled us aside and said cryptically, "Be careful; the vines will talk to you." I realized later that she was alluding to John 15:5, where Jesus talked to his disciples about the vine and the branches, that only by abiding in him could they produce fruit. At the time, I simply smiled and nodded awkwardly. It sounded a bit weird to me, but I assumed her heart and intentions were good.

After a handful of us—including my wife and ten-year-old son, Jeremy—listened to Tracey's short tutorial, we started pruning. I quickly realized a couple of things.

First, this was going to be actual work. For a half hour or so, it was like a scene from a movie. But after the sun rose higher in the sky and our sweat was dropping to the ground, it became apparent that this would be an exhausting and, if we didn't hurry, all-day affair.

I also came to realize that pruning is a ruthless act. In my mind, I had confused pruning a rose bush and pruning a vineyard. A little snip here and a little snip there and we'd be through. But vineyards typically hang on trellises that are six feet high. And when you prune them, you massively cut the excess branches down to a fraction of what they were beforehand.

You look for branches that have no buds, and you cut them. Some of the branches I cut were eight to ten feet long, and it didn't feel right. I kept asking Nico, Tracey's son, "Is this right? It feels like I'm killing this vine." And he kept saying, "You're not killing it. You're making room for the sunlight to get to the branches that actually have buds and will produce grapes."

As Tracey predicted, the vines were already speaking to me. While I cut away the vines, I reflected on all the pruning the Father had done in my life. His pruning felt like a ruthless act—at times, like he was killing me. But he wasn't. He was cutting and pruning the sins and distractions of my soul so that the light of his Son could produce rich fruit in and through me.

While I worked, my thoughts drifted back to many of the trials I had faced: fatherlessness, violence, isolation, fear, near-death experiences, a ministry financial crisis, and more. God used all of them to cut away my self-reliance and pride.

As the heat of the Italian sun beat down, I couldn't get the words of Jesus out of my mind: "I am the vine, you are the branches. He who abides in Me and I in him, bears much fruit; for without Me you can do nothing" (John 15:5, NKJV).

LESSONS FROM THE VINEYARD

Following our experience in the Italian vineyard, I spent some time studying John 15 in more detail. The context in which Jesus shared this lesson with his disciples was after he had washed their feet on the night of his betrayal. It was after the Last Supper, where he visually and viscerally demonstrated his broken body with bread and his shed blood with wine.

Perhaps he was on his way to the garden of Gethsemane with

his disciples that night and passed by a vineyard just like the one we had pruned. Picture him pausing by the vineyard and using it as an analogy for the key to spiritual growth and gospel impact.

Jesus abruptly turned to his disciples and declared, "I am the true vine, and my Father is the gardener. He cuts off every branch in me that bears no fruit, while every branch that does bear fruit he prunes so that it will be even more fruitful" (John 15:1-2).

They must have been baffled, trying to understand the analogy. Jesus, sensing their confusion, continued: "Abide in Me, and I in you. As the branch cannot bear fruit of itself, unless it abides in the vine, neither can you, unless you abide in Me" (John 15:4, NKJV).

Jesus used the Greek word *meno* seven times in John 15:1-8. It means a deep enduring. Some translations use the word "remain" instead of "abide," but both words capture Jesus' meaning. Like a guest who refuses to leave a house, we must refuse to leave Jesus. We must be the houseguest who never leaves. The great thing is, he wants us to stay. He *commands* us to stay.

We are to abide in Jesus as he abides in us. He declares, "Remain in me, as I also remain in you" (John 15:4). Did you catch that? Our standard for abiding is Jesus. Just as Jesus comes to dwell inside us through his Holy Spirit at the moment of salvation and never leaves, so we are to abide in him perpetually, continually, relentlessly.

In his classic book *True Spirituality*, Francis Schaeffer calls this "active passivity."[1] We actively rely on Jesus to live through us. Or, as R. J. Koerper, my former youth ministry professor at Colorado Christian University, used to call it, "a moment-by-moment daily declaration of dependence on Jesus."

Major W. Ian Thomas, the founder of Torchbearers evangelism training centers all over the world, learned this secret early in his ministry. He had a slogan that became a hallmark of his approach to living the Christian life: "Lord Jesus, I can't, You never said I could; but You can, and always said You would. That is all I need to know."[2]

So many times we strain in our flesh to start, stop, restart, commit, recommit, and *re*recommit ourselves to Christ. We end up like Peter, disowning Jesus with our lives and lips by sinful decisions made or by refusing to share the gospel.

When Jesus turned toward Peter after his final denial, we're told that Peter "went out and wept bitterly" (Luke 22:62, NKJV).

Peter had forgotten to abide in Jesus. Instead of remembering Jesus' words in the garden of Gethsemane to "watch and pray so that you will not fall into temptation" (Matthew 26:41), Peter and crew fell asleep.

They forgot to remain. They forgot to abide. Minutes earlier they had heard Jesus' analogy of the vineyard and his relentless reminder to remain in him. And still they fell asleep.

But something happened on the Day of Pentecost that changed everything. The Holy Spirit came to abide in them. Acts 2:1-4 paints the picture beautifully:

> When the day of Pentecost came, they were all together in one place. Suddenly a sound like the blowing of a violent wind came from heaven and filled the whole house where they were sitting. They saw what seemed to be tongues of fire that separated and came to rest on each of them. All of them were filled with the Holy Spirit and began to speak in other tongues as the Spirit enabled them.

Not only were Peter and crew able to spontaneously speak the gospel in other languages, but they were also filled with a holy boldness. Before Pentecost, the Holy Spirit was with them. Now he was in them. Jesus had predicted this. Speaking of the Holy Spirit, he had said, "But you know him, because he lives with you now and later will be in you" (John 14:17, NLT).

After Pentecost the apostles were able to abide in Christ by relentlessly relying on his indwelling Holy Spirit. As a result, Jesus produced fruit through them, and they were changed men. Acts 4:13 puts it this way: "When [the members of the Sanhedrin] saw the courage of Peter and John and realized that they were unschooled, ordinary men, they were astonished and they took note that these men had been with Jesus."

Ordinary people become extraordinary—dare I say radical—when they learn the secret of abiding in Christ. Because when they do, it will no longer be them living, but Christ living through them.

The great apostle Paul had his own way of putting it: "I have been crucified with Christ and I no longer live, but Christ lives in me. The life I now live in the body, I live by faith in the Son of God, who loved me and gave himself for me" (Galatians 2:20).

THE HAND AND THE GLOVE

What does abiding look like in the twenty-first century? How does abiding help us live a radical life?

My friend Zane Black, a former drug dealer, is one example. Zane went into a coma on the bathroom floor of a movie theater after overdosing. Yet through the grace of God, he was radically transformed by the gospel of Jesus Christ and enrolled at a Bible school, where he began to grow deeper in his faith. It was there he learned from the teachings of Major W. Ian Thomas about how to abide.

When I first met Zane a couple decades ago, I was blown away by his story. He had a childhood innocence and a new believer's passion. He had taught some devotionals at the school but was not seminary trained. He had never preached a sermon in front of a large audience.

But he was an abider. He depended on Jesus, and it was evident.

ABIDE

So I invited him to give his testimony at one of our conferences. He was willing but terrified.

But Zane killed it—actually, Christ through Zane killed it. The teenagers were deeply moved, and many made decisions for Christ. Today, Zane travels with Dare 2 Share and speaks at our events. He is one of the premier youth speakers in America.

Why? He abides in Jesus, and Jesus lives and speaks through him.

Zane uses an analogy with teenagers to explain what it means to abide in Christ. As an avid mountain biker, he owns some pretty torn up mountain biking gloves. He brings one of them out and flops it down on the podium. "This is a glove," he says to the teenagers. "It can't do anything. It just lays there."

"This is my hand," he says, holding up his hand with his fingers spread out. "When I put my hand in the glove, it's almost as though the glove comes alive. It can do what my hand can do. If I make my hand into a fist, the glove moves into the shape of a fist. If I pick something up with my hand, the glove does the same. Why? It's not the glove. It's the hand in the glove.

"What's true of the glove is true of us. In and of ourselves, we can do nothing. But Jesus is the hand. He abides in us, just like my hand abides in this glove. We can do anything Christ can do because it is him working through us!"

May you abide in Christ as he abides in you. May you allow him to live through you.

The fateful lesson on that faith-shaking night when Jesus was betrayed by Judas is one the disciples remembered for the rest of their lives.

Church history tells us that ten of the remaining eleven disciples died as martyrs. Clearly, they absorbed Jesus' lesson on how to abide in Christ. They lived it until their dying day. So must you.

Let the vines talk to you.

I set my watch alarm to ring three times a day to remind me to abide in Christ. I ask him to fill me with his Spirit and live through me.

Set reminders throughout the day to abide in Christ. You can set a vibrating alarm on your smartwatch, have a reminder pop up on your calendar, use sticky notes in prominent places, or hire someone to run up behind you and yell "abide" three times per day.

Take the challenge. Abiding in Christ is the secret to a Christian life that is radical like Jesus.

16

WRESTLE

Being in anguish, he prayed more earnestly,
and his sweat was like drops of blood falling to the ground.

LUKE 22:44

"LET'S WRESTLE, DAD!" my five-year-old daughter, Kailey, routinely declared when I came home from work or from a trip.

Dropping my bags, we would fake wrestle for a few minutes. Then she would "throw" me to the ground, and I would fall down in fake pain. She would jump on my stomach with a move that would make Hulk Hogan proud. Recovering, I would "throw" her to the ground. On and on we went until one of us pinned the other and was counted out.

Sometimes she would win and sometimes not. But it would always be an exciting match.

This went on year after year after year. One day when I came home from a trip, my now twelve-year-old daughter met me at the door and challenged me. "Let's wrestle."

But now my "little Kailey" had grown into a preteenager. She seemed a little too old for these fake wrestling matches. So later that night I asked my wife about it. "Kailey wanted to wrestle today. But she seems a little too old for that now, don't you think?"

My kindhearted wife just rolled her eyes at me and said, "Come on, Greg. That's just her way of being close to you."

I will never forget her statement. Having wrestled throughout middle school and high school, I knew this to be true. You are never closer to someone than when you are wrestling with them.

Take a look at Olympic wrestlers. When they engage their opponent, they're fully focused with every fiber of their being. They are locked in, intertwined, straining for the angle, pushing for the leverage, and usually a big sweaty mess.

Take a look at my favorite Old Testament wrestler, Jacob, and his mysterious wrestling match with a stranger in the middle of the night. They were locked in, intertwined, and straining for the angle in an all-night wrestling match.

WRESTLING WITH JESUS

Genesis 32:24-26 paints a vivid picture:

> Jacob was left alone, and a man wrestled with him
> till daybreak. When the man saw that he could not
> overpower him, he touched the socket of Jacob's hip so
> that his hip was wrenched as he wrestled with the
> man. Then the man said, "Let me go, for it is daybreak."
>
> But Jacob replied, "I will not let you go unless you
> bless me."

This passage is just plain weird. A guy shows up out of nowhere in the middle of the night when Jacob is all by himself and picks a fight.

What makes this story even weirder is that a few verses later Jacob makes it clear that the opponent he was wrestling was God himself: "Jacob called the place Peniel, saying, 'It is because I saw God face to face, and yet my life was spared'" (Genesis 32:30).

I think this scene represents a Christophany, a preincarnate appearance of Christ in the Old Testament. Long before Jesus Christ showed up as God-in-the-flesh on earth, he showed up as God-in-a-wrestling-uniform in this passage. Someone declared verbally or nonverbally, "Let's wrestle." And wrestle they did. They wrestled until daybreak. They wrestled until Jacob was a sweaty mess. They wrestled until Christ touched Jacob's hip and his socket was wrenched from its place, and he was injured. They wrestled until Jacob got what he wanted.

We don't know if Jacob had the Son of God in a headlock, leg lock, arm bar, or some other ancient power move. But we do know that Jacob was determined to get blessed by God in this so-crazy-that-it-must-be-true biblical story.

And that's exactly what happened:

The man asked him, "What is your name?"

"Jacob," he answered.

Then the man said, "Your name will no longer be Jacob, but Israel, because you have struggled with God and with humans and have overcome."

GENESIS 32:27-28

From that day on Jacob walked with both a limp and a smile. From that day Jacob had a new name and all the blessings that came with it. It was worth using a cane.

Fast-forward 1,600 years, and we see another wrestling match unfold. One wrestler is the same, Jesus. But who is his opponent this time? Not Jacob, but God the Father. It is "Hell in a Cell" in the garden of Gethsemane as Jesus wrestles with his Father in prayer.

To fully understand this wrestling match, we need to revisit the theological truth of the humanity of Jesus. Two thousand years ago, Jesus became one of us, fully God and fully human. That means he experienced real hunger (see Matthew 4:2) and real thirst (see John 4:7). That means he got tired (see John 4:6) and experienced real human emotions.

Nowhere is his humanity seen more clearly than in the garden of Gethsemane. Amid olive trees and sleeping disciples, Jesus faced his worst nightmare. It was not the beating that awaited him by the Temple guards, not the horrific flogging at the hands of the Roman soldiers, not even the excruciatingly painful crucifixion he would soon suffer that shook him the most.

What Jesus dreaded more than anything was the anticipation of experiencing the wrath of his Father for the first time in all eternity. He knew he would soon experience God's wrath for the sin of humanity when he hung on the cross in our place and because of our sins.

For all of eternity past, all that the Son of God had ever experienced from the Father was 100 percent pure love. Remember how the Father declared, "This is my Son, whom I love; with him I am well pleased" (Matthew 3:17)? That was just a snapshot of how the Father had felt about the Son for eons before the creation of the earth.

But in just a few short hours, that never-ending ocean of love that had been poured out on Jesus by the Father would be exchanged for the cup of God's boiling wrath. This may be hard for many to comprehend. How can God be loving and wrathful at the same time?

Although God is love (see 1 John 4:8), he is also holy, set apart completely from sin (see Isaiah 6:3). Although he loves us, he hates sin. He hates it to the point of utter wrath. Why? Because sin devastates everything it touches. It devastates lives. It devastates families. It has devastated this world again and again. It seeks to devastate God's glory. It is contrary to everything about his character and his plan. That's why God's wrath toward sin is boiling. And it was God's boiling cup of wrath toward sin that was about to be poured out on the Son of God when he died in our place on the cross.

So Jesus desperately prayed, asking God for a way out, looking for an escape clause in the atonement contract. And this wasn't just praying but crying, not just crying but weeping, not just weeping but sweating, not just sweating but bleeding.

Hematidrosis is a rare medical phenomenon that can happen when someone is in so much stress and anguish, their capillaries burst and they literally sweat blood. This was Jesus in the garden of Gethsemane: "Being in anguish, he prayed more earnestly, and his sweat was like drops of blood falling to the ground" (Luke 22:44).

For three hours, 180 minutes, 10,800 seconds, Jesus prayed the same prayer again and again. He prayed, "Father, if you are willing, take this cup from me; yet not my will, but yours be done" (Luke 22:42).

What was this cup Jesus was talking about? It was God's cup of wrath.

In the Old Testament it was God's cup of wrath that was poured out on the disobedient Israelites (see Jeremiah 25:15-16; Isaiah 51:17, 22; Lamentations 4:21). In the end times, the seven-year Tribulation—when everyone on earth endures unimaginable suffering—is an example of God's cup of wrath being poured out on a disobedient world. In Revelation 14:10-11, everyone in hell will be forced to drink of the cup of God's wrath forever in the form of fire and brimstone.

Jesus didn't want to taste this cup of wrath. That's why he

prayed, "Father, if you are willing, take this cup from me." He knew what was coming and was praying for another option.

He shuddered at the thought of suffering his Father's wrath—this one he had loved and who loved him from eternity past. The thought traumatized Jesus so much, he literally sweat blood.

Jesus, in the garden of Gethsemane, was in a wrestling match between his humanity and God's will. He desperately called out to God for three hours that fateful night for another way to pay the price for sin. But there was no other way.

So after three hours of wrestling in prayer, Jesus tapped out. He surrendered to the Father and said, "Yet not my will, but yours be done."

After that, according to bestselling author Philip Yancey, Jesus was the calmest person present at his trials.[1] Why? He had wrestled with the Father and was fully surrendered to do his will, despite the cost, despite the pain.

But this was not Jesus' first wrestling match with the Father. It may have been the most intense one, but it was not the only one.

Hebrews 5:7 makes this clear: "During the days of Jesus' life on earth, he offered up prayers and petitions with fervent cries and tears to the one who could save him from death, and he was heard because of his reverent submission."

TAPPING OUT TO GOD

During Jesus' three-and-a-half-year earthly ministry, and maybe before, he wrestled with the Father in prayer. He prayed "with fervent cries and tears." He prayed with passion and intensity. He prayed for God's will to be done in his life, ministry, and coming death.

As a result of this wrestling, a revolution began—a revolution of radically changed lives and saved souls. This wrestling with

God in prayer has produced radicals like Jesus for the last two thousand years.

Martin Luther wrestled with God in the sixteenth century over *sola fide*—whether we are saved by faith plus works or faith alone in Christ.

Nineteenth-century missionary to China Hudson Taylor, having been temporarily paralyzed by a fall and unsure if he would make it back on the mission field, wrestled with God over the workers that needed to be raised up to shake China for God.

Twentieth-century missionary to India Amy Carmichael wrestled with God in prayer over the spiritual fate of the Indian people.

The wrestling matches continue to this day. They have with me. They have with my daughter, Kailey, who is nineteen years old now.

Kailey loves Jesus with all her heart. She is a spiritual leader at her school and a phenomenal worship leader and songwriter. Kailey is an unashamed witness for the Lord Jesus Christ.

But from the time she was a young teenager, Kailey has struggled with anxiety. Our sweet girl has had many bouts of debilitating anxiety, sleepless nights, tear-filled conversations with Mom and Dad, and some counseling over her battle with her neurotic nemesis.

One day she asked me, "Dad, why does God allow this anxiety to attack me? Why doesn't he just take it away?"

I looked at her and said, "Kailey, what has this anxiety caused you to do?" She thought about it for a moment and said, "It has caused me to turn to God, to read his Word, to memorize Bible verses, and to pour out my heart to him in prayer and songwriting."

"In other words," I responded, "this anxiety has caused you to wrestle with God."

She nodded. And I reminded her of her wrestling matches with me and her mother's response when I asked her about it.

Looking into her eyes, I said, "Kailey, God has allowed you the privilege of wrestling with him in prayer because it is his way of being close to you. When you are struggling with him, he has you wrapped up in his arms, and you are closer than ever."

I could see in her eyes that my statement spoke to her in the depths of her soul.

I pray it speaks to you as well.

Perhaps you are wrestling with anxiety, the death of a loved one, or the loss of a job. Maybe you are struggling with fear, anger, regret, shame, or sin.

Whatever you are wrestling with, just remember to wrestle with God in prayer.

When you wrestle physically on a consistent basis, you get stronger and more limber. Wrestling with God in prayer does the same thing. It makes you stronger spiritually and more limber in life.

But most importantly, it gets you close to God.

Imagine him standing in your doorway right now, declaring, "Let's wrestle." Because he is.

RADICAL LIKE JESUS CHALLENGE #16
Difficulty: Medium

Find a quiet, isolated place (preferably outside) and wrestle with God in prayer for an hour over a specific challenge, problem, or crisis you are facing. Pray out loud. Remember the words of Jesus to Peter in Matthew 26:40-41: "Couldn't you men keep watch with me for one hour?... Watch and pray so that you will not fall into temptation. The spirit is willing, but the flesh is weak."

17

SUFFER

And they crucified him.

MARK 15:24

THE FOUR SIMPLE WORDS "and they crucified him" don't catch the full impact of Christ's suffering in the hours leading up to his crucifixion.

They don't even come close.

Wrapped in a blanket of darkness amid the olive trees of the garden of Gethsemane, Jesus wrestled with and ultimately submitted to his Father's will. Then he heard distant footsteps coming toward him. Between the twisted branches of the olive trees, he watched the torches flicker as those coming to arrest him grew closer. He was betrayed by Judas Iscariot with a kiss on the cheek. Moments later his friends would flee into the darkness of night, and before the break of dawn, his go-to leader would disown him three separate times.

TRIED

That night Jesus was arrested. Over the next several hours he would endure six trials—three religious and three civil—but all outrageous.

During one of these kangaroo courts, he was blindfolded, spat upon, mocked, slapped, and punched again and again. As he stood there blindfolded, those who slapped him taunted him by yelling, "Who just hit you? Come on! You're a prophet? What's my name?"

Imagine the Son of God, bloodied, beaten, his face dripping with spit from a whole crew of mockers, from the very humanity he had created.

But Jesus never fought back. Although he could have called down lightning to destroy them all or dispatched an army of angels from heaven to wipe them out, he took every punch, every slap, and every false accusation.

Eventually, he stood before Pontius Pilate, the Roman governor who had the power to free him or crucify him. Pilate wanted to release him, but the Jewish religious leaders stirred up the crowd until they demanded Jesus' death, repeatedly yelling, "Crucify him! Crucify him!"

Finally, Pontius Pilate gave in to the crowd and handed Jesus— the only truly innocent one who ever lived—over to be crucified.

That's when the physical suffering began.

TORTURED

Romans were experts at execution. They knew how to torture criminals with maximum pain. And they really wanted to make an example of Jesus, who some were calling the King of the Jews. To the Romans there was only one king—Caesar. They would show this Jewish "king" (and all his followers) who the real boss was.

It started with a beating. Not just any beating, but one that carried the nickname "the half death," because half the people who experienced it died from it.

Jesus was stripped of his clothes and most likely chained to a stone pillar, where Roman soldiers used a cat-o'-nine-tails to whip him over and over and over again. A cat-o'-nine-tails is a handle with nine strands of leather attached. Metal balls were woven into the leather, and pieces of broken pottery, glass, razors, and twisted metal, designed to grab and rip flesh, were fastened to the end of each strand.

Imagine Jesus being flogged over and over and over and over again, with huge pieces of skin and muscle ripped and torn away with every blow. By the time the torturers were done, his back and buttocks and legs were nothing but bloody ribbons of flesh and muscle and sinew.

The Romans knew how to bring their victims right to the point of death through blood loss, right to the edge of the cliff between life and death before they pulled back. That's exactly what they did with Jesus.

But they weren't done with the torture after flogging him. They mocked him by placing a purple robe on him because purple was the color of royalty.

But a king is not a king without a crown. These bloodthirsty soldiers wove together a crown of thorns. Don't mistake these for the tiny thorns on a rose bush. These were Jerusalem thorns, and they were two to three inches long and sharp as a spike. After the soldiers beat him to a bloody pulp, they shoved this barbarous crown on his head. Imagine for a moment what it would feel like as the sharp tips from these thorns went deeper and deeper into his forehead and all around his skull.

Then they beat the thorny crown into his skull with a rod. They hit him over and over in the face. Isaiah prophesied that this beating would be so bad, Jesus wouldn't even look human by the time it was over (see Isaiah 52:14).

TORMENTED

Having beaten him to an unrecognizable bloody pulp, the soldiers knelt before him and mocked him by screaming, "Hail, King of the Jews!" They kept spitting and slapping, hitting and harassing. The torment he endured was unthinkable.

But Jesus never resisted or said an unkind word to them. He absorbed every punch without anger. He marinated in their saliva with no malice in his heart toward his accusers.

At some point, according to Isaiah's prophecy, Jesus had his beard ripped from his face (see Isaiah 50:6). He was a mangled mess by the time they were done with him.

Once they had mocked him enough, they stripped him of the purple robe. By then the blood on his back and legs had dried and was no doubt caked to the robe. Like a Band-Aid that covered his shoulders, back, buttocks, and legs, the robe was ripped away, with pain reverberating through every molecule of his body. The previously coagulated blood flowed again.

Soon after, the soldiers replaced the robe with a huge wooden cross and forced him to carry it outside Jerusalem to the place of crucifixion.

But it was too much even for Jesus. Once a strong carpenter who had lugged many pieces of wood from forest to town, he had now lost so much blood that he crumpled under the weight.

Angrily, the soldiers grabbed a man from the crowd and forced him to carry the cross.

Once on top of Golgotha, the hill of the skull, the crucifixion took place.

The Roman soldiers stripped Jesus of all his clothes, threw him down on the wooden cross, and stretched out his hand. They took a spike nail and hammered it relentlessly into his wrist. Imagine the pain with each blow as the hammer came down again and again.

Then they repeated the process with his other wrist. Why his wrists? Because a nail through the palm would not support the weight of his body once lifted up. The spike would quickly tear through his hand, and he would fall down from the cross. However, there are two bones in the wrist that come together and provide a solid anchor for the spikes to support a full-grown man.

After his wrists were spiked, his feet were brought together and a large nail was driven through both his feet.

Imagine Jesus' screams as each of these blows hit the nail deeper and deeper into his flesh and muscle and ligaments. Imagine the excruciating shock waves of pain that reverberated through his body.

Jesus wasn't cheating. He didn't use his God powers to turn off the pain receptors in his brain. He refused to drink the offered wine mixed with gall that would deaden his senses and numb his pain.

No, Jesus was willing to experience the full cup of God's wrath, taking our place with no Novocain chaser. He chose to suffer fully in our place in order to forgive our sins fully.

Once Jesus was nailed to the cross, the soldiers lifted it up and dropped it into a hole. It was probably at this point that, according to Psalm 22, all his bones came out of joint. The jolt of that huge wooden cross being dropped into a hole would make bones pop out of their joints, and the pain would be excruciating.

To breathe on the cross was no small thing. A crucified person had to push up to exhale and come down to inhale. That's why, when it was time for a crucified person to die, Roman soldiers would break their legs. Then the crucified person couldn't push up anymore and they would suffocate, no longer able to breathe.

Imagine the open, bloody back of Jesus scraping against the rough-hewn wood of the cross for hours as he struggled to breathe, his open wounds embedded with splinters and every nerve raw with electrifying, unimaginable pain.

If there was a pain scale from 1 to 10 for those who suffered a Roman crucifixion, it would be a 10 every time. It was a slow, painful, humiliating death. Victims hung naked and twisted, nailed to a cross of wood before a mocking crowd.

Added to Jesus' suffering was the reality that most of his friends had deserted him.

Given the loss of blood from the Roman flogging, his facial disfigurement from the relentless beating of the powerful soldiers, and the cup of wrath that his beloved Father would soon pour out upon him, no one in the history of humanity has ever suffered more.

Every time I take Communion and crunch the cracker between my teeth, I think of the crunch of those angry fists against his innocent face. Every time I feel the Communion juice flow down my throat, I think of the blood of Jesus flowing down his face, back, hands, feet, and side as he died in my place because of my sin. I think of the old hymn's words:

Jesus paid it all
All to him I owe
Sin had left a crimson stain
He washed it white as snow.[1]

Our sins have been washed away through his blood. We can now stand before the thrice-holy God, clothed in the righteousness of Christ, which was given to us by Jesus in exchange for our sin at our moment of faith.

But if we're honest, we know that we still struggle with sin. We may be eternally forgiven, but on earth we still fight the flesh. We battle with selfishness. Maybe we harbor secret sins.

So how does God help purify us from the sins that, although we are eternally forgiven for them, we may still struggle with on this earth?

The answer is suffering.

The apostle Peter explains the role of suffering when it comes to the sanctification of the believer: "Therefore, since Christ suffered in his body, arm yourselves also with the same attitude, because whoever suffers in the body is done with sin. As a result, they do not live the rest of their earthly lives for evil human desires, but rather for the will of God" (1 Peter 4:1-2). Peter tells us that we must "arm" ourselves with the same attitude Jesus had when it comes to suffering. And how did Jesus arm himself? At first, he wrestled with the Father in the garden of Gethsemane, asking God to deliver him from it if there was a way. But, as God made it clear that there was no other way, Jesus said, "Your will be done."

With that phrase he armed himself. With that phrase we can arm ourselves when it comes to the trials and troubles we are facing. We may start with prayers for deliverance but, as it becomes clear that this is suffering the Father wills us to endure, we proclaim with Jesus, "Your will be done."

But Peter gives more than a command; he gives a reason: "Because whoever suffers in the body is done with sin. As a result, they do not live the rest of their earthly lives for evil human desires, but rather for the will of God."

The suffering of Christ and his death on our behalf cleanses us from our sin positionally before God, but the suffering we endure on this earth can cleanse us from sins practically in our lives. It's like a soap that purifies us. It's like the sculptor's chisel that chips away the excess to reveal a masterpiece underneath.

GOD SCULPTS A MASTERPIECE OUT OF OUR PAIN

God allows the hammer blows of pain to reverberate through that chisel of suffering placed against the sins and self-absorption we all have in our lives. He uses this pain to carefully sculpt us into the image of Christ.

I think of my friend Jane Dratz, who has been my internal editor at Dare 2 Share for the last eighteen years. During a four-year period, Jane was diagnosed with three different primary cancers—one of which was stage 4. Recently, she's battled a fourth primary cancer. The five-year survival rate for her stage 4 cancer was 15 percent, and her doctors told her bluntly they would try hard to get her five more years.

But Jane didn't want to live her remaining days in sadness and despair, waiting to die. Instead, she chose to actively model how to face hardship, suffering, and even death with faith in the goodness of God. She determined to allow the Holy Spirit to use this cancer like a chisel to chip away any areas of her life that didn't please him and to turn her into a masterpiece crafted in the image of Christ.

So far, God, in his grace, has granted her life. It's been fourteen years since her stage 4 cancer diagnosis. She lives with confidence in the God she trusts, continuing to use her gifts for impact in God's Kingdom while knowing that her days are numbered by the Lord. (Yours and mine are too. She's just more aware of that truth than most of us.)

I can tell you personally that I know of no other person who has more of a passion for God and a desire to please him in every way. Every second she lives is like a sacrifice of praise offered on the altar to God. The pain of her suffering has accelerated her passion for God and desire for holiness, not dampened it. She lives her life not for her own "evil human desires, but rather for the will of God."

Perhaps it's not cancer you are suffering from. Maybe it's a financial trial, a strain in your marriage, the pain of not finding someone to marry, a son or daughter who is wayward, a struggle with loneliness or anxiety that is all consuming, or something else.

Whatever it is, think of Jesus and the unfathomable pain he endured on the cross on your behalf. Imagine him using this trial to purify you, sanctify you, and draw you closer to him.

Then, like Jane, thank God it is bringing you nearer to him. This Jesus, who experienced more pain and suffering than you or I could ever imagine, is with you and for you and by you as you walk through it. And he is using it to make you more like him.

RADICAL LIKE JESUS CHALLENGE #17
Difficulty: Medium

In the space provided, write a "suffering account" of your life to God. Think through the five biggest trials you have faced since becoming a Christian and describe how each of those trials has brought you nearer to him, cleansed you from sin, and made you more like Jesus.

FORGIVE

Jesus said, "Father, forgive them,
for they do not know what they are doing."

LUKE 23:34

IF YOU'VE EVER WALKED THROUGH the Holocaust museums in Jerusalem or Washington, DC, you will never be the same. My family and I left the DC museum stunned and dumbfounded by the cruelty of Hitler and the Nazi regime. That feeling was intensified when we visited the Dachau concentration camp outside Munich, Germany.

Every step across Dachau felt both sacred and sickening. It's almost as though we could still hear the screams, feel the suffering, and smell the stench of death that permeated the place more than eighty years before.

As we walked through these Holocaust museums and later through Dachau, my thoughts wandered back to *The Hiding Place*, the 1975 movie based on the life and concentration camp imprisonment of Corrie ten Boom and her family. Watching that movie deeply impacted me as a teenager. Witnessing the faith of this woman grow deeper and deeper amid unimaginable suffering made my heart long for a Christian faith like hers.

Corrie and her family were arrested by the Nazis for hiding Jews in their home. She and her sister, Betsie, were sent to Ravensbrück concentration camp, where they suffered horrific atrocities. But instead of giving way to anger or abandoning their faith, the sisters cared for, comforted, prayed for, evangelized, and discipled their fellow prisoners. Their underground ministry impacted lives, and many prisoners turned to the Lord.

Betsie died just a few days before Corrie was released from the camp. After the war, Corrie established a home of healing for other camp survivors and traveled the world preaching about God's forgiveness.

At one of these speaking events in Munich, she came face-to-face with a Ravensbrück prison guard who had subsequently become a Christian. This guard had been in charge of the bathroom. When the women had to take off their clothes, he and his fellow soldiers mocked them cruelly. Although he was now a Christian, Corrie was sickened at the sight of him.

When he approached her, the ex-guard thanked her again and again for the message she had shared. He asked for her forgiveness and extended his hand. But Corrie froze. She knew that Jesus had forgiven him. Still, as she tried to extend her hand to grasp his, she just could not will herself to forgive. Silently she prayed, "Jesus, I cannot forgive him. Give me your forgiveness." And then with tears in her eyes she uttered the shackle-shattering words: "I forgive you, brother."

Here's how she described what happened next:

As I took his hand the most incredible thing happened. From my shoulder along my arm and through my hand, a current seemed to pass from me to him, while into my heart sprang a love for this stranger that almost overwhelmed me. And so I discovered that it is not on our forgiveness any more than on our goodness that the world's healing hinges, but on His.[1]

If Corrie ten Boom discovered the secret to forgiveness after the intense and unspeakable suffering she and her sister endured in a concentration camp, then so can we.

THE SECRET TO FORGIVING OTHERS

The secret to truly forgiving others is understanding how much it cost for God to forgive us.

When Jesus hung upon the cross and prayed, "Father, forgive them, for they do not know what they are doing" (Luke 23:34), he wasn't just speaking of the Roman soldiers who crucified him or the Jewish leaders who turned him over to the Roman authorities to be crucified.

He was speaking of us.

It was our sins that drove him to the cross. It was your sin and mine. As the prophet reminds us,

> He was pierced for *our* transgressions,
>   he was crushed for *our* iniquities;
> the punishment that brought *us* peace was on him,
>   and by his wounds *we* are healed.
> *We all*, like sheep, have gone astray,
>   *each of us* has turned to *our own* way;
> and the LORD has laid on him
>   the iniquity of *us all*.

ISAIAH 53:5-6, EMPHASIS ADDED

The Roman soldier's hammer that drove the nails into his hands and feet is in our right hand, and the spear that pierced his side is in our left hand. Our fingerprints are all over the scene of the crime. We are guilty because it was our sins that drove him to his death.

But on the precipice of death, he prayed for us. And after he prayed pleading for our forgiveness, he paid the price to make it happen.

In Matthew 27:45-46, we read, "From noon until three in the afternoon darkness came over all the land. About three in the afternoon Jesus cried out in a loud voice, '*Eli, Eli, lema sabachthani?*' (which means 'My God, my God, why have you forsaken me?')."

Why did Jesus cry out these words in a loud voice? Because in that moment God the Father poured out on Jesus the full measure of his wrath for humanity's sin. For the first time in the history of the eternal, there was a tremor in the Trinity as God emptied the cup of his wrath on his one and only Son whom he loved. God's Son took our place and bore the punishment for our sins.

And moments later he spoke the words that would change the course of humanity: "It is finished" (John 19:30). With those words he bowed his head and died.

The price of our sin had been paid in full on the cross of Christ. Jesus offered himself as a perfect sacrifice in our place. As a perfect human, he could die for other humans. As God, that payment was infinite and eternal.

Jesus didn't just *pray* for our forgiveness; he *paid* for our forgiveness with his own blood.

And because he forgave us, we can forgive anyone, for anything.

WHEN A NIGHTMARE BECOMES A REALITY

Sometimes this brand of forgiveness strikes close to home. It did for me when I struggled to forgive my biological father for abandoning my ma and me before I was even born.

It struck again for my wife and me just a handful of years ago when our son, Jeremy, was a senior in high school. I'll never forget the night he barged into our bedroom at one in the morning.

"Dad, I have to tell you something," he said with an urgency that roused me from a dead sleep.

Sitting up slowly, I mumbled, "What, Jeremy?"

He rattled off a string of rapid-fire statements that quickly got my attention and reverberated like a fire alarm inside my soul. "I have something to confess to you," he said. "I can't live with myself any longer. I have to tell you something!"

Now fully awake, I asked nervously, "What is it?"

Jeremy explained that during the previous school year, he had been secretly vaping, getting drunk, and getting high on marijuana with his friends. Somehow he had kept it a secret from his mother and me. Even though she was a public school teacher and I had worked with teenagers for most of my adult life, he had somehow pulled the wool over our eyes for months.

He went on to explain that he had quit all his vices a long time ago but also admitted that he couldn't bear keeping the secret any longer. His conscience had been tortured by the conviction of the indwelling Holy Spirit, and he needed to confess.

Then he asked me a premature question. "So what are my consequences?"

I said, "Jeremy, you woke me in the middle of the night and dumped all this on me. Your mom and I are going to need some time to process this. But I can tell you the first consequence. We have to go downstairs and wake up your mom and tell her."

My wife, Debbie, was an elementary school teacher, and during the school year, about 30 percent of the time, she fell asleep downstairs by the fireplace while grading papers. This was one of those nights.

So Jeremy and I took the slow march of death down the stairs to wake her up and break the bad news to her.

It wasn't pretty.

She was rightfully upset. Her precious, innocent boy wasn't so innocent after all. The rest of that night was long and painful, full of tears and screams and questions, but mostly tears. We were on that couch for hours, trying to take it in and figure out next steps.

Again, Jeremy asked, "What are my consequences?" He was especially worried that I would go to his Christian school administration and turn him in for breaking the honor code. If I did, he explained, they would expel him. And that terrified Jeremy.

He was also nervous because he understood that I'm a by-the-rules dad. When they were kids, if either my son or daughter disobeyed, Debbie and I would give them immediate consequences. The only counting we did was counting up the number of punishments they would be receiving for their disobedience.

Finally, just before dawn, I answered his question. "Your mom and I never saw this coming," I said. "We need time to process through what the consequences should be. We are going to take two weeks to pray and think about it. We want to get this right. After we pray through and decide, then, and only then, will we sit down and tell you your consequences."

Those two weeks of waiting were part of the consequence. Jeremy was worried and nervous and kept asking what we were going to do. We would just say, "You'll have to wait and see." Debbie and I were genuinely conflicted. She has more mercy than I do. I wanted to bring the full weight of the law down on him for his acts of rebellion.

I say "acts" because it was more than just alcohol, vaping, and drug use. He had broken the law by illegally buying drugs from a drug dealer. He had, in a very real sense, stolen from us during that time by having us transfer money for food into his account. But the money wasn't for food. After looking through my bank records over those months, I saw that I had transferred at least $500 into his account over the course of six months or so. What I had written off as teenage appetite was actually funding his vices.

Jeremy had broken the law, school rules, house rules, and our hearts—as well as God's. It became increasingly clear that he deserved the most extreme consequences we could muster.

Three days before we were scheduled to let Jeremy know what we were going to do, God gave us the answer we had been praying for.

THE ONE WORD THAT CHANGES EVERYTHING

On "judgment day," we sat down at the kitchen table with Jeremy to unpack the severity of his consequences. Earlier that day I had taken a blank sheet of paper and filled it with all the rules and laws he had broken with his rebellion. I wrote down all the potential consequences we could choose—getting the police involved, grounding for a year, letting the school know he had broken the honor code, and making him pay back the $500 with interest and penalties.

The paper was completely full of sins committed, rules broken, and consequences pending.

I said, "Jeremy, look this sheet over and tell me if we got all this right."

His face drained of color. He briefly glanced at it and said, "Dad, just tell me my consequences."

I said, "No. Read this paper in full and make sure everything is completely accurate."

Jeremy slowly read every word on the paper before handing it to me with his head down. "Yes, Dad," he said somberly, "everything is accurate. Those are the things I did wrong. Those are the punishments I deserve. Now please tell me what my consequences will be."

With that I took the piece of paper full of sins and consequences and placed it squarely in front of me. I reached for the black Sharpie on the table and wrote one word in big, black letters across the paper: *TETELESTAI*.

He looked at it and said, "I have no idea what that word means."

I said, "It's what Jesus said on the cross when he died. It's the Greek word for 'it is finished' and 'paid in full.' It was what merchants used to stamp on a bill that had been fully paid."

He looked at me blankly and said, "Dad, I know Jesus forgives me for my sins. I'm not worried about him. I'm worried about the consequences you and Mom are going to give me."

Then I leaned across the table and put my hand on his shoulder. Looking into his eyes, I said, "Jeremy, you're not picking up what I'm putting down. Here's your consequence: there is no consequence. You came to us. You confessed. So we are completely forgiving you. We are not going to turn you into the school. We are not going to ground you or even make you pay back the $500 you stole from us. You are completely, 100 percent forgiven."

You could almost see the burden fall off Jeremy's back. And that was the beginning of his turnaround.

Today, Jeremy is married to a godly woman and has made it his life goal to please the Lord in everything he says and does.

Forgiveness changed everything for him. Our act of forgiveness toward our son was just a tiny snapshot of the enormity of the forgiveness Jesus prayed for and paid for on the cross for us.

We could forgive Jeremy because we had been forgiven by Jesus.

Maybe someone has wronged you. Maybe they hurt you.

Perhaps they didn't steal $500 from you but stole your innocence, that promotion you worked so hard for, or your childhood by breaking up your family with an affair.

Whatever it is, just remember this: because Jesus forgave us, we can forgive anyone for anything, no matter what.

Who is that person you need to forgive?

A decade ago, as we walked through Dachau, being reminded of the horrific suffering the Jews endured during the Holocaust, the sound of a large bell began to reverberate across the courtyard. I asked our tour guide, "What is that sound?"

"That's the three o'clock bell," he said, pointing across the grounds to a giant bell erected on the far end. "After the Holocaust, Christian survivors came back to Dachau and erected a giant bell that would ring at three o'clock every day."

"Why three o'clock?" I asked.

His answer shook me to the core. "Because Jesus died at three o'clock. And in the midst of this painfully horrific reminder of the Holocaust, these Christians wanted the world to know that Jesus suffered and died to purchase their victory on the cross."

What a beautiful picture!

Amid the hell of hurt you have suffered at the hands, words, or actions of someone else, can you hear the bell ring? It's ringing the sound of victory. It's ringing the sound of forgiveness. It's ringing the sound of *tetelestai*!

If you have put your faith in Jesus based on his death on the cross, you are forgiven. And if you are forgiven, you can forgive anyone for anything, through the power of the ultimate Forgiver who dwells in you—Jesus!

Just like Corrie ten Boom, ask Jesus to help you forgive that person, then do it! You may have to do it a thousand times more after that, but it starts with the first time.

Who has hurt you the most? Write a letter of forgiveness to him or her and send it, if appropriate. If not, hold on to it and reread it every time you feel the bile of bitterness rise up in the back of your throat.

19

DIE

Unless a kernel of wheat falls to the ground and dies,
it remains only a single seed. But if it dies, it produces many seeds.

JOHN 12:24

IT WAS A LATE SATURDAY AFTERNOON IN MARCH. I stood on the stage at Faith Bible Chapel with tears streaming down my cheeks, mourning a death . . . the death of a dream.

Ever since I was a teenager I had doodled stadiums full of people. My dream was to be like Billy Graham and preach the gospel to thousands of people. As I grew older, that dream crystalized into envisioning arenas full of teenagers being inspired, equipped, and unleashed to share the gospel.

And by God's grace, I had lived that dream. For twenty-five years I had been blessed to mobilize a generation to gospelize their world through the ministry I had founded, Dare 2 Share. We had filled large churches, conference centers, and arenas across the United States with teenagers. And at every single event, after we trained teenagers to share the gospel, we turned them loose to go do it.

A vice president at Dare 2 Share once asked me if there might be a better way to train teenagers to share the gospel and to consider letting go of these large events. I glared at him with a stare that would have made William Wallace nervous and growled, "You can have the Dare 2 Share conferences when you pry them from my cold, dead fingers."

I was right. I had to die—to myself—for the conferences to die.

So that Saturday afternoon I was attending the funeral of my dream. The conferences had finally been pried from my cold, dead-to-myself fingers.

But from that death sprang new life. Since that fateful funeral on March 25, 2017, God has allowed that dead seed to produce many seeds. Now, instead of city-by-city events, we do a global day of youth evangelism called Dare 2 Share Live that mobilizes teenagers around the world to share the gospel in one twenty-four-hour span. Now thousands of teenagers and churches participate. Our faith-sharing app is available in nineteen languages, and our training curriculum has been downloaded in over 90 percent of the countries on the planet. Because of God's relentless blessing, we are partnering with key ministries around the world, working together until "every teen everywhere hears the gospel from a friend."

ARE YOU READY TO DIE?

Jesus said, "Unless a kernel of wheat falls to the ground and dies, it remains only a single seed. But if it dies, it produces many seeds." But then he added, "Anyone who loves their life will lose it, while anyone who hates their life in this world will keep it for eternal life" (John 12:24-25).

What is the life that you must hate? What is the dream that you must die to? Are you ready to follow the path of Jesus, the *Via Dolorosa*, the way of suffering? Are you ready to die?

Jesus was.

John 19:30 puts it poetically, but it was death nonetheless: "When he had received the drink, Jesus said, 'It is finished.' With that, he bowed his head and gave up his spirit."

Jesus willingly died on the cross, even though he was entitled to rule and reign with a power that would leave no doubt about his being the King of the universe. But instead of being seated on a throne, he was nailed to a cross. Instead of wearing a crown of gold, he wore a crown of thorns. Instead of a signet ring on his finger, he had nails through his wrists. Instead of a scepter in his hand, he had a spear in his side.

Here was our King—bruised and broken, drenched in blood, covered in flies.

But as Jesus taught, unless the kernel of wheat dies, it won't produce seeds. Today, because of his death, some two billion seeds around the world claim the name of Christ.

Jesus died, and he bids us, as believers, to come and die to ourselves.

This was not Jesus' first call to his disciples. Jesus called them to "repent and believe." And after they became believers, he gave them his final call of full-on discipleship—to "come and die."

Once you have put your faith in Jesus and received his free gift of life, Jesus begins to help you die—to yourself, to your dreams, to your sin.

In a sense it is a one-time death. Paul refers to it in Galatians 5:24: "Those who belong to Christ Jesus have crucified the flesh with its passions and desires."

When you put your faith in Jesus, your sins are forgiven—past, present, and future. This is a legal, positional, and heavenly reality. When God sees you, he sees you as a saint, a holy one. Even though the Corinthian believers struggled with all sorts of sin, including internal strife and division, pagan idolatry, and the grossest forms of sexual immorality, God viewed them through cross-colored lenses. Paul addresses them as "the church of God in Corinth, . . . those sanctified in Christ Jesus and called to be his holy people ['saints']" (1 Corinthians 1:2).

He viewed them as sanctified, as saints, as holy ones who needed to live up to who they were in Christ. So if they were dead to their sin, why did they still struggle with sin? Or an even better question is, why do you?

REACHING FOR YOUR CROSS

In one sense dying to yourself is a one-time death. In another sense, it's a daily death. Jesus put it this way in Luke 9:23: "Whoever wants to be my disciple must deny themselves and take up their cross daily and follow me."

In ancient Roman culture, when you saw someone carrying their cross, you knew exactly what that meant. They were on their way to be crucified.

Every morning when you wake up, before you pour your first cup of coffee, before you even yawn and stretch, you must reach over the edge of your bed and feel for the cross you must pick up that day.

Some days that means dying to a dream.

Some days that means dying to a particular sin.

Some days that means dying to your selfish tendencies.

Some days that means dying to your reluctance to speak about Jesus.

Some days that means all of the above.

When you die to yourself, you can multiply your impact.

I saw it multiply through the death of our Dare 2 Share conferences.

Jesus saw it multiply through his death, resulting in billions of believers added to heaven's rolls.

Aisha saw it multiply through her own death.

AISHA'S STORY

Dare 2 Share has a ministry partner in Africa we'll call Jacob (to protect his identity). He's a Kenyan national, and he uses Dare 2 Share training material across his continent to mobilize teenagers for the gospel. He often travels to dangerous places for his job, places where sharing the gospel is illegal. But Jacob is both determined and strategically shrewd.

One trip took Jacob to Zanzibar, an island in East Africa known for persecuting Christians. He flew there to meet with Christian teenagers and equip them to share their faith using the Life in 6 Words app. Jacob was nervous about this very dangerous venture because it is against the law in Zanzibar for Christians to share the gospel with Muslims and seek to convert them.

When he first arrived on the island, he got lost, so he asked a teenage girl for directions. The teenager was a charming, kind-hearted Muslim girl who knew exactly where the location was. She introduced herself as Aisha and offered to take him there herself.

Along the way, she asked Jacob what the meeting was about. He hesitated for a moment, knowing that if he shared too much, it could get him in trouble. After all, he was there to train Christian teens to share their faith. He told Aisha it was a gathering of Christian young people who were excited about God. When she asked if she could attend the meeting, he got even more nervous. But she was so kind and sincere that he gave in and told her she was welcome.

When Aisha walked into the meeting, she was blown away

by the energy and excitement in the roomful of Christians. Jacob introduced her around.

After the meeting started, Jacob had the young people download the Life in 6 Words app onto their phones and showed them how to use it. He told them if they could swipe and read, they could share the gospel.

Jacob instructed all the teenagers to break up into pairs and start practicing sharing the gospel using the app. Aisha was in one of the practice groups, and the Christian teenager she was paired with took her through the app and shared the gospel in the process, role-playing a gospel conversation.

After the Christian teen had swiped through all the GOSPEL slides, the final slide popped up. It read, "Are you ready to place your faith in Jesus?" The girl showed it to Aisha, who said she was ready and pushed the button.

The girl didn't know if Aisha was role-playing or serious, so she asked, "Did you really just now put your faith in Jesus?" With a huge smile on her face, Aisha affirmed she had indeed trusted in Jesus.

Aisha's practice partner called Jacob over and explained what had just happened. Jacob went over the gospel with Aisha again to make sure she had truly understood the message, and she had! In that moment of faith, Aisha's life was radically transformed. She had never known that God loved her. She had always seen Allah as a demanding god who was hard—even impossible—to please. But now she knew Jesus. Now she knew that "God so loved the world that he gave his one and only Son, that whoever believes in him shall not perish but have eternal life" (John 3:16). Now she knew love and hope and peace.

Aisha became unstoppable. Using all she had learned from the meeting, she started boldly sharing the gospel. Evangelism is a capital offense in Zanzibar, but Aisha didn't care. She just *had* to get the Good News to her friends.

Some of them believed in Jesus but others refused, calling her a *kafir*, an Arabic word meaning "infidel" or "deserter."

Within a day, Aisha was arrested and taken to the Sharia court. She was given twenty-four hours to renounce her faith in Christ. She refused.

The Muslim authorities asked her if she had any last requests. She had only one. She asked for permission to write a goodbye letter to her friends and classmates. The Muslim authorities consented.

That was a mistake. Because in that letter she wrote about how Jesus had radically transformed her life. She shared how she heard the Good News that Jesus loved her and that it changed everything for her. She shared the message of the gospel she had learned from the Life in 6 Words app. She begged her friends and classmates to believe in Jesus and be rescued from the hopelessness they were steeped in without Christ.

As her letter circulated, first among her friends, then among her classmates, and finally among the community, many people came to Christ. Some fled the country. Others were persecuted. But all who trusted in Christ were transformed.

Revival broke out in Zanzibar because of one teen who was radically transformed by the gospel and then showed apostolic resolve to advance it to her friends.

A mere twenty-four hours after being sentenced, Aisha—this brand-new believer—was brought to the town square. The people of the town gathered around her, picked up big rocks, and stoned her to death.

Aisha died as a modern-day martyr. She died with the same holy resolve as Stephen, the first martyr of the church.

And her death accelerated the revival even further across Zanzibar.

She, like a kernel of wheat, died, but her death produced countless seeds across Zanzibar. Her story continues to inspire Christians around the world.

Aisha was willing to literally die for her faith. What are you willing to die to in your life?

RADICAL LIKE JESUS CHALLENGE #19
Difficulty: Medium

Go to a local graveyard, wander around, and read the gravestones for at least thirty minutes. Then, in a quiet part of the graveyard, have your own funeral service for something that you need to die to. Maybe it's your reluctance to share the gospel with a certain person. Maybe it is a sin that has been dominating you. Maybe it is a general narcissism that is controlling your attitude. Perhaps it is lingering bitterness over someone who hurt you deeply. Whatever it is, visualize it buried in that graveyard once and for all.

20

RISE

In their fright the women bowed down with their faces to the ground,
but the men said to them, "Why do you look for the living among the dead?
He is not here; he has risen!"

LUKE 24:5-6

THE TENSION FILLING OUR CAR that night was so thick, you could have cut it with a knife. My wife and I, married only five years at the time, were on the way to our couple's Bible study. En route, a horrendous argument had erupted between us. As we pulled up to the house, nothing was resolved. If anything, our argument had descended into a no-holds-barred accusation fest.

We sat in the car trying to resolve the problem before we dared join the others. As couples walked by, we whisper-yelled, hoping they wouldn't catch on that we were in full-on fight mode.

But our thorny problem had roots that reached way too deep to be pulled out in a few minutes. It had been spreading its tentacles deep down into the soil of our relationship for years, and yanking it out would take more strength than Debbie and I collectively had. Besides, I don't think I really wanted to pull it out. Uprooting this nasty weed would be difficult—even painful—and it would create a mess. I just wanted to neatly cut it off at the top and make everything look good to all outward appearances.

One thing I did know was that we had to get into the Bible study shortly after start time. Why? Because I was the pastor of the church!

Six years earlier I had planted the church with my good friend Rick Long. A few years after that, I started Dare 2 Share. Both were growing. It seemed like every night was busy (elder meetings, counseling, church events, etc.). Every day was busy (sermon prep, writing content for Dare 2 Share, ministry meetings, etc.). Every weekend was busy, either doing Dare 2 Share conferences or preaching Sunday sermons. My time with my wife had been crowded out by what she called my mistress—"Ministry."

In my mind at the time, this was just the sacrifice she was called to make "for the sake of the cause." In her mind, she had married someone who was not keeping his vow to "love, honor, and cherish her."

Sitting in the car, neither of us budged from our opinion. In fact, things were getting even more intense.

Finally, out of exasperation, I said, "Well, put on a happy face. We're going in!"

But my wife was not happy at all. She didn't want to go in, but after a few "we'll deal with this laters," she finally caved and reluctantly walked in with me.

As soon as we walked through the door, we went our separate ways. I worked the room, faking a smile the best I could but still fuming underneath.

By the time we grabbed some coffee and snacks and gathered in the big Bible study circle, I had calmed down a bit. But Debbie was strangely quiet, which was fine with me. The last thing I wanted was for the tension between us to leak out in front of our Bible study.

Thank the Lord I was not leading the Bible study that night. The associate pastor was. As we settled into our seats ready to dive into our study, he casually announced, "Tonight, instead of going through the Bible study, why don't we just go around the room and see how we are doing spiritually and as couples? Let's be real, raw, and honest."

My heart dropped like an anchor in the ocean. *Oh crud,* I thought to myself. *How am I going to spin this?*

As person after person and couple after couple shared, I didn't hear a word of what they were saying. I was plotting how I could share just enough to be truthful, just enough to satisfy my wife, but not so much that I'd embarrass her (or myself) or make people think we had a real problem in our marriage.

Call me the spin doctor.

"BLAH, BLAH, BLAH . . ." BOOM!

When it was my turn, I talked about the "busyness of ministry" and the "ongoing quest to find the perfect work-life balance." I said, "Pray for us as we find our rhythms in life and marriage." Blah, blah, blah.

Then it was Debbie's turn to share. I wasn't worried. Although she is a fifth-grade public school teacher, she is naturally shy. She was (and still is) a beloved fixture in Arvada, Colorado, the suburb of Denver where we live. She is *that* teacher that kids remember, beloved by all who know her. Unlike me, she has no natural predators—except Satan.

The associate pastor asked, "So, Debbie, how is it going?" I knew I was in serious trouble when she all but yelled, "Not good!"

Everyone's head turned toward her in full attention as the group leader asked the inevitable follow-up question, "Why? What's going on?"

And then Debbie, like a volcano that had been dormant for years, began spewing angry words like hot lava across the room.

"My husband is gone every weekend! He's gone every night! When he is home, he's got nothing left for me! He just falls asleep watching television! He doesn't communicate with me! I can't take it or fake it anymore! My husband is a jerk!"

Nobody had ever seen Debbie angry like this, and jaws dropped open as all eyes turned to me. But I was beyond embarrassed. I was enraged.

I screamed back, "You want to do this now in front of everyone? Well, let's get it on!"

And we were off, continuing the argument from the car, but this time there was no whisper-yelling. We screamed at each other—no filters, no holding back.

I think most people thought it was some kind of skit. I had done some crazy stuff before in church just to make a point.

But this was no skit. This was a full-on, everything-but-fists verbal fight of fury.

She accused me of being married to the ministry, of not making time for her, of not loving her like Christ loved the church.

I accused her of not being willing to endure me being gone for the sake of the lost souls that were being won and lives that were being changed.

Then the associate pastor interrupted our argument. He looked at me and said, "I don't care if you're pastor of the largest church in America. I don't care if Dare 2 Share reaches every last teenager on the planet. If you don't take care of business at home and love your wife like you should, all of it is for nothing!"

Now my crazy eyes turned toward him with a steely gaze of rage. I rose to my feet and yelled, "You may be right, but I'm going to take you out!"

With clenched fists I lunged across the Bible study circle toward him in a full rage. The Bible study attendees now could be certain that this was no skit. You could feel the air sucked out of the room as I picked out which part of his jaw I was going to smash. I figured I had already sinned by neglecting my wife. If I was going to get fired from the church, I was going to go out in style by knocking a fellow pastor out cold.

But in the middle of the room, I was the one who was almost knocked out. The Holy Spirit must have been waiting for me with his own clenched fist in the middle of the Bible study circle. I dropped to the shag carpet, curled into a fetal position, and began to weep—not cry, but weep and wail. In that moment I knew that Debbie was right, and the associate pastor was right. I had overlooked my wife and my marriage. I had put the ministry above everything and everyone—including Jesus.

I wept and stayed curled in that fetal position for thirty minutes. I wailed and cried and was, for the first time in my life, truly inconsolable. Everyone gathered around me and prayed as I wept.

During those 1,800 seconds, I died to myself. When I finally stood up, face and chest drenched in tears, I knew something had to change, and I knew something would. My standing up was like a resurrection from the dead.

RESURRECTION POWER

I knew the theological answer to the question of how to die to myself and live for Christ before my meltdown, but I had not applied it in my marriage. The answer was resurrection power.

The same power that raised Jesus from the dead could raise my marriage from the dead, could bury my selfishness and raise the new and reborn Greg Stier from the dead. Bible verses began to flood my mind. Verses like this one:

> I pray that the eyes of your heart may be enlightened
> in order that you may know . . . his incomparably great

power for us who believe. That power is the same as the mighty strength he exerted when he raised Christ from the dead and seated him at his right hand in the heavenly realms, far above all rule and authority, power and dominion, and every name that is invoked, not only in the present age but also in the one to come.

EPHESIANS 1:18-21

Be strong in the Lord and in his mighty power.

EPHESIANS 6:10

I want to know Christ—yes, to know the power of his resurrection and participation in his sufferings, becoming like him in his death, and so, somehow, attaining to the resurrection from the dead.

Not that I have already obtained all this, or have already arrived at my goal, but I press on to take hold of that for which Christ Jesus took hold of me. Brothers and sisters, I do not consider myself yet to have taken hold of it. But one thing I do: Forgetting what is behind and straining toward what is ahead, I press on toward the goal to win the prize for which God has called me heavenward in Christ Jesus.

PHILIPPIANS 3:10-14

Think about this. The same power that raised Jesus from the dead is available to us as believers. Paul prays in Ephesians 1 that our eyes would be opened to that theological reality. In Ephesians 6 he commands us to live in that power. In Philippians 3 he tells us to "press on to take hold" of that reality.

If we learn to die to ourselves and live in his resurrection power, there is not a marriage that cannot be saved (if both are seeking to live in resurrection power). There's not an addiction that cannot be broken. There's not a sin or habit that cannot be conquered.

But this doesn't mean that it will be easy or automatic. As the apostle Paul announced in frustration in Romans 7:15, "I do not understand what I do. For what I want to do I do not do, but what I hate I do." This was Paul *after* he was saved! He still struggled, but he fought through to break through, which is what we read a few short verses later in Romans 7:21-25:

> I find this law at work: Although I want to do good, evil
> is right there with me. For in my inner being I delight
> in God's law; but I see another law at work in me,
> waging war against the law of my mind and making me
> a prisoner of the law of sin at work within me. What a
> wretched man I am! Who will rescue me from this body
> that is subject to death? Thanks be to God, who delivers
> me through Jesus Christ our Lord!

Through the resurrection power of Christ, you, like Paul, can struggle through until you reach breakthrough!

When Jesus rose from the dead, it was a powerful event. Matthew 28:2-4 describes it like this:

> There was a violent earthquake, for an angel of the Lord
> came down from heaven and, going to the tomb, rolled back
> the stone and sat on it. His appearance was like lightning,
> and his clothes were white as snow. The guards were so
> afraid of him that they shook and became like dead men.

It was so powerful that the big, tough, expert-at-fighting Roman soldiers convulsed and passed out on the spot. They "shook and became like dead men."

When we walk in resurrection power, in a sense, our biggest sins and addictions seize up and pass out. What about Satan? James 4:7 tells us, "Submit yourselves, then, to God. Resist the devil, and he will flee from you."

When we submit to God, get full of the resurrection power of Christ, and resist the devil in Jesus' power (not our own), the evil one runs like Forrest Gump in the opposite direction.

So how do we walk in resurrection power? We yield to his indwelling Holy Spirit. We ask him to take control. As soon as we do, it is Christ himself living through us. Now, if you're like me, this is something you will have to do repeatedly throughout the day.

Think of this power like a plug-in outlet and not jumper cables. Too many Christians go to church or Bible study and get hooked up to the preacher or Bible study leader's jumper cables to get a jolt that will last them through the week. The problem is, after a while, this kind of power dies like a weak battery.

Instead, plug into the steady current of resurrection power always available to you by just asking God to fill and fuel you throughout the day.

As Paul wrote in Galatians 2:20, "I have been crucified with Christ and I no longer live, but Christ lives in me. The life I now live in the body, I live by faith in the Son of God, who loved me and gave himself for me."

This verse has been an anchor for my soul and my marriage for over three decades now. It's his resurrection power that didn't just save our marriage but transformed it.

It can transform you as well. Let the Holy Spirit fill you. Let the person of Christ live through you and the power of the resurrected Christ flow through you. Walk with a holy swagger over your sin and the struggles in your life, marriage, work, and ministry.

Plug in to his resurrection power.

Memorize Galatians 2:20. Then go on a long walk, meditating on the reality that Christ lives in you. Close out your walk by listening to the song "Same Power" by Jeremy Camp on a streaming app or online.

21

MULTIPLY

Jesus came to them and said, "All authority in heaven and on earth has been given to me. Therefore go and make disciples of all nations, baptizing them in the name of the Father and of the Son and of the Holy Spirit, and teaching them to obey everything I have commanded you. And surely I am with you always, to the very end of the age."

MATTHEW 28:18-20

I HAD HEARD THE HYPE that once you visit the Holy Land, you'll never be the same. You will no longer read Scripture in black and white but in living color.

The hype is true.

Visiting Israel was a game changer for me.

I was there along with 180 ministry leaders from 53 countries. All these ministry leaders were focused on disciple-multiplying. Most of them were intent on mobilizing the next generation to lead the way.

We walked the Wadi Kelt, the Judean wilderness where Jesus was tempted by the devil after forty days of fasting. We visited the holy sites in Jerusalem. We checked out "the gates of hell" in Caesarea Philippi and sailed across the Sea of Galilee to "the other side," where the demoniacs lived.

The Dead Sea was overrated. The roadside figs were delicious.

But the highlight for me was Mount Arbel. Many believe this was the mountain where Jesus gathered his disciples and delivered the great commission. The setting is dramatic. Rising 1,200 feet above the Sea of Galilee, it is the tallest mountain in the area. Its eastern-facing cliff drops straight down toward the sea, providing a panoramic, full-color backdrop to many of the events described in the Gospels.

From the edge of the cliff, the disciples could have seen where Jesus walked on the water, calmed the sea, fed the five thousand, preached the Sermon on the Mount, restored Peter after his denials, and more. On the distant horizon they could also see some of the "all nations" Jesus was calling them to go and make disciples in.

As a guy with an active imagination, I envisioned the disciples gathered around Jesus near Mount Arbel's eastern cliff. I imagined him, with the amazing backdrop of the Sea of Galilee behind and below, telling them, "All authority in heaven and on earth has been given to me. Therefore go and make disciples of all nations."

But he tagged on to that command a few extras that are often overlooked.

He also commanded the disciples to baptize those who believed the gospel. This act steels and seals a new believer's faith as they publicly identify with Jesus and his death, burial, and resurrection through baptism. It doesn't save them, but it does mark them as a follower of Jesus.

But Jesus didn't stop there. He had one more command to go with this commission. He told them to teach these new believers to "obey everything I have commanded you." This, of course, included the command to go and make disciples.

In other words, this passage is actually about not just making but multiplying disciples.

This multiplication effect is what took the gospel from Jerusalem to Rome in less than thirty years without planes, trains, or Instagram. Jesus ascended to heaven in Acts 1. In Acts 2 the disciples were filled with the Spirit and their tongues set on fire for the gospel. As a result, "three thousand were added to their number that day" (disciples made; Acts 2:41), and you can be sure that those three thousand were telling their family and friends about this Good News they had embraced (disciples multiplied). By Acts 6 it's clear that disciples were everywhere in Jerusalem. "The word of God spread. The number of disciples in Jerusalem increased rapidly, and a large number of priests became obedient to the faith" (Acts 6:7). Newly converted believers were spreading the gospel, and it became an unstoppable force.

What started with a core group of twelve disciples has now multiplied into a global movement that is present in every country in the world. Over the last two thousand years, billions have been reached through the power of disciples made and multiplied.

And now Jesus' call is in your hands and mine. Yes, we are both called to multiply disciples. You may be thinking, *Well, you're a preacher. Isn't multiplying disciples your job?* Yes, it is. But it's just as much your job. It was my job long before I was a preacher—back when I was nailing shingles as a roofer. I made and multiplied disciples then. I make and multiply disciples now.

Are you? This great commission—or the Cause, as I like to call it—is just as much for you as it was for the early disciples or as it is for me. God has strategically placed you in a family, in a circle of friends, in a neighborhood, at a job or school to multiply disciples. To love the people around you enough to share the Good News of the gospel and create disciples who make disciples.

You cannot be radical like Jesus if you are not willing to multiply disciples.

Yet many Christians are intimidated by the idea of sharing their faith and making disciples. They think it feels too pushy or too judgmental or too controversial. But none of those things need be true if you share the Good News in a clear, loving, relational way. The key is to draw your courage and convictions directly from Jesus and his love for all humanity.

Here are three truths that will help motivate and mobilize you.

TRUTH #1: THE RIGHT TO MULTIPLY DISCIPLES

Let's take a closer look at the wording of Jesus' command to go. "Then Jesus came to them and said, 'All authority in heaven and on earth has been given to me. Therefore go and make disciples of all nations'" (Matthew 28:18-19).

Jesus was reminding his disciples that he had been given authority over the entire universe, seen and unseen. He had authority over nature, for he calmed the wind and the waves with a word. He had authority over sickness, for he healed a leper, a blind man, a paralytic, and countless hundreds, if not thousands, more. He had authority over death, for he raised Lazarus after four days in the grave. He had authority over demons based on the many episodes of demons being catapulted out of souls with a flick of his divine finger.

All authority in heaven and earth had been given to Jesus—therefore *go*.

This means you have the right to multiply disciples because Jesus has commanded you to do so.

You have the right to bring up the gospel, explain it, try to gently persuade others to believe it, and help them grow and multiply once they do.

There are those in this culture who declare you don't have the right to try to change someone else's beliefs. Yet changing one's mind is the very essence of repentance. In fact, the Greek word for repentance, *metanoia*, literally means "to change one's mind." This is exactly what Peter called the crowd to do in Acts 2:38—to repent, to change their minds about who Jesus is and how to be saved. Peter was later arrested and called before the Sanhedrin, the same Jewish leaders who turned Jesus over to be crucified months earlier. Acts 5:28-29 describes the scene:

> "We gave you strict orders not to teach in this name,"
> [the high priest] said. "Yet you have filled Jerusalem with
> your teaching and are determined to make us guilty of
> this man's blood."
>
> Peter and the other apostles replied: "We must obey
> God rather than human beings!"

In essence, Peter and the others told the Jewish leaders that they had the right to multiply disciples. The King of kings, Jesus himself, had given them this right.

You have the right to multiply disciples too.

TRUTH #2: THE RESPONSIBILITY TO MULTIPLY DISCIPLES

As someone once said, it's called the great commission, not "the good suggestion." It's not optional. It's not just for those, like me, with the gift of evangelism. It's for everyday Joes and Jolenes. It's for every believer.

It's for you.

How do you begin to do this? There's a simple process that can help you called Prayer-Care-Share.

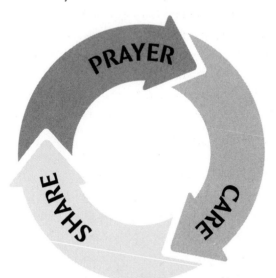

To start, write the name of someone you know who needs the gospel in the center of the circle. Start praying daily that they would come to faith in Jesus. Start caring for them in tangible ways. Then, at the appropriate time, share the gospel with them. Use the GOSPEL acrostic or the Life in 6 Words app mentioned in chapter 9. Once they trust in Jesus, encourage them to pray for, care for, and share with one other person.

When I was a pastor, we had a rule at our church. If you led someone to Jesus, you could baptize them. On one memorable occasion, I was backstage before the service with the three individuals about to be baptized—one adult and two teenagers. I was going to baptize the adult, Dave, because I had led him to Jesus and discipled him. I just assumed he had recently led both the teenagers to Christ and was planning on baptizing them. But that was not their plan! We had four generations of believers present! I had led Dave to Christ, and Dave had led one teenager to Jesus, and then that teenager had led the other teenager!

This was disciple multiplication at its finest!

When you start purposefully praying for, caring for, and sharing the gospel with others around you, you'll be surprised what happens. Then as those in your circle of influence say yes to Jesus, challenge them to do the same within their own circle of influence.

TRUTH #3: THE RESOLVE TO MULTIPLY DISCIPLES

Multiplying disciples takes courage. So where do you get the resolve—the determination and tenacity—to do it? From the promise that Jesus goes with you. In Matthew 28:20 he told his disciples, "And surely I am with you always, even to the end of the age."

Let that sink in for a moment. The King of the universe, the Savior of the church, Jesus himself, goes with you everywhere you go.

If you were with your best friend from out of town and walked up to a group of your friends, you wouldn't hesitate to introduce your best friend to your other friends. Then why would you hesitate to introduce your *best* of best friends, Jesus, to your friends, neighbors, coworkers, family, classmates, and yes, maybe even strangers?

The promise that Jesus goes with you should inspire you with unstoppable courage! The maker of heaven and earth is with you when you are being mocked for sharing the gospel. And he is there when you introduce someone to their Savior.

He will give you the power to proclaim and the wisdom to do it in a loving and effective way. He will help you make disciples. He will empower you to multiply disciples. I've seen God do this firsthand with the shyest teenager I have ever met. Her name was Kathy.

When I was a middle school youth leader at Community Baptist Church in Arvada, Colorado, Kathy was a part of my youth group. She usually stood quietly in the corner or whispered a conversation with her friends. She would barely make eye contact when I talked to her, always looking down or away. Kathy was a sweet girl, just painfully shy.

Week after week I talked to these middle schoolers about the resolve it takes to share your faith at school. I equipped them to share the gospel and reminded them that they were not alone as they walked the hallways of their public schools. Jesus went with them.

I challenged them to be bold, but I also gave them a weekly opportunity to put their boldness into action.

A large group of us went out to local shopping malls every Friday night to share the gospel with teenagers who were hanging out there. Kathy never wanted to go. Week after week I challenged her. Week after week she declined.

But one night after youth group I all but begged her, adding that if she came, she wouldn't need to say anything. She could just stand there and pray while I did all the talking.

She finally, reluctantly, agreed.

That next Friday night when we arrived inside the mall, we split up into pairs to look for teenagers we could talk to about the gospel. Kathy paired up with me.

With each encounter, I did all the talking and Kathy stood about five feet behind me and prayed. It was going pretty well until we walked up to three high school girls sitting in the middle of the mall on a bench. I said, "Hi, my name is Greg, and this is Kathy." Middle schooler Kathy was standing five feet behind and barely looked up at them when she gave a nod and smiled shyly.

"I want to ask you a question," I continued. "If I could tell you in a few minutes how you could know you were going to heaven when you die, would that be good news?"

The leader of the pack said, "Yes, it would be." But then she got a sly smile on her face. "But we don't want to hear it from you. We want to hear it from her," she said, pointing to a now terrified Kathy.

A chill went down my spine. An electrical shock went down Kathy's.

I'll never forget looking back at Kathy and watching something miraculous unfold. One instant she was trembling, with her head down in fear and embarrassment, but in the next instant she lifted her head with a look of holy resolve. In that moment she remembered the words of Jesus: "I am with you always." She realized Jesus was with her and the power of the Holy Spirit lived inside her. And with a confidence I had never seen in her before, she took five steps forward and shared the gospel the way she had been equipped to. And those three girls said yes to Jesus in the middle of the mall that amazing night.

Whether you are shy like Kathy or bold like Peter, the Holy Spirit will fill you with a holy resolve that will enable you to go and make disciples. He will make you radical like Jesus.

RADICAL LIKE JESUS CHALLENGE #21
Difficulty: Hard

Make *and* multiply disciples.

Make: Prayerfully place the name of one person in the Prayer-Care-Share circle on the following page. Start with prayer and care, and then when the time is right, share the gospel.

Multiply: Prayerfully identify and invite one Christian to go through *Radical like Jesus* with you. Let the truths you learned and applied from the life of Jesus in the pages of this book multiply in and through another person. Call them and set your first meeting in the next seven days.

Two Final Challenges

CHALLENGE #1:
DON'T UNDERESTIMATE THE NEXT GENERATION.

Sprinkled throughout this book are stories of young people who lived radical-like-Jesus lifestyles. Some of that emphasis is because I was relentlessly challenged to do radical things for Jesus when I was a teenager. Some of it is because I have been mobilizing teenagers to share the gospel for thirty-plus years and have a vision of "every teen everywhere hearing the gospel from a friend" (all one billion of them) in my lifetime. Some of it is because I believe Jesus mobilized mostly teenagers to be his disciples (see Matthew 17:24-27 and Exodus 30:14-15), Paul mobilized a young man named Timothy to follow in his footsteps (see 1 Timothy 4:12), and God has mobilized teenagers to launch spiritual awakenings for the last two thousand years.

In the words of my friend Kathy Branzell, the president of the National Day of Prayer, "Teenagers are not the *next* generation, they are the *now* generation."

Nobody can be more radical like and for Jesus than teenagers! Their bodies are full of adrenaline and hormones. Their brains aren't fully developed. They are looking for a mission to live for and a King to die for. If all of that can be harnessed and focused on Christ and his cause, then they, through the Holy Spirit's power unleashed within them, can be an unstoppable force for change.

Encourage the young people in your sphere of influence (kids, grandkids, nieces, nephews, etc.) to go all in to follow Jesus. Challenge them to live radical lives for the glory of God and the advancement of his gospel. And most of all, pray that God would do a mighty work in them so that he can do a radical work through them.

CHALLENGE #2:
KEEP LIVING A RADICAL JESUS LIFESTYLE!

As you've taken on the twenty-one challenges throughout this book, you've stepped outside your comfort zone by doing things you've never done before. Hopefully, these obedience-based actions have shaped your character and deepened your faith as you've been increasingly forged into the image of the radical Jesus found in the pages of Scripture.

But don't stop now. Keep reading the Gospels and analyzing what Jesus did and taught. Ask God what the equivalent action would be for you. Then do it! Do this with the whole of Scripture, not just with the red letters of the Gospels, for he inspired the entire Bible (see 2 Timothy 3:16).

Do what he did. Live like he lived. Love like he loved. Preach like he preached. Serve like he served. Die like he died and rise like he rose—in victory over sin and Satan!

In closing, join me in praying this prayer out loud:

Dear Father,

Thank you for sending your Son. Thank you that his radical love and life changed the world for all eternity.

Thank you for changing me through the insights and challenges in this book. But may I not stop here. May I *start* here. Show me how to model my life after Jesus on every level so that Christ in and through me would empower everything I do. May those I encounter who are hurting be healed. May those I encounter who are lost be saved. May those I encounter who are sad find joy.

Make me radical like Jesus every day, in every way.

In the name of Jesus I pray, amen.

Acknowledgments

WRITING A BOOK IS NO EASY TASK, especially for the spouses of OCD authors like yours truly. I want to thank my one-of-a-kind bride, Debbie, for her patience with me as I trounced off into the wilderness (quite literally) to write this book. Often, when I write, I resemble Jack Nicholson in *The Shining* (minus the axe and menacing grin) and just type and type and type for hours on end in a cabin up in the Rocky Mountains near where we live in Denver. My wife has mastered the routine of agreeing to my multiple-times-a-year cabin getaways so that I can finish a book project like this. I am so grateful for her patience with my many writing retreats. I hope that she knows full well that she is reaping a reward in heaven for the ongoing sacrifices she makes for the sake of the gospel.

I also want to thank Debbie Bresina, the president of Dare 2 Share and longtime coconspirator in crimes against the forces of darkness. We have mobilized teenagers for the cause of Christ side by side for three decades now. This book, in many ways, was her idea. I'll never forget the day she sat me down in her office and said, "Write a book for me." I was like, "For you personally?" After giggling at my genuine misunderstanding, she said, "No, for a person like me.

Write a book for a Christian man or woman, like me, who wants to take it to the next level spiritually." Soon after, the idea for this book erupted. Debbie has been the nitrogen to my glycerin. The ideas we've created together over the last thirty-plus years, by God's grace, have been explosive.

Thanks go to Jane Dratz as well. Although Jane has had many health challenges over the years, she has always done her best to make time to edit my work. There are few people I trust like Jane. She loves the Lord, knows the Word, has the boldness to call me on stuff, and understands my writing voice and what I'm really trying to communicate. Although she has not been on Dare 2 Share staff for years, I am super grateful she is willing to edit my books in retirement.

To Tyndale, especially Jon Farrar, Jonathan L. Schindler, and crew, I am super grateful for your hard work on this project. Your inventive ideas and genuine excitement for the message of this book have been so energizing. It has been an honor to work with Tyndale as a publisher.

To my agent, Don Gates, I am blessed by your always-honest assessment of book ideas and writing style. You speak the truth in a loving way, and you make things happen.

Last, but not least, I want to thank the staff, board, and donors of Dare 2 Share. Your commitment to the cause of Christ has given me a steady stream of encouragement to keep calling everyone to be radical like Jesus!

Notes

CHAPTER 1: BE

1. James Clear, *Atomic Habits* (New York: Avery, 2018), 38.

CHAPTER 2: GROW

1. Roy B. Blizzard and David Bivin, "Study Shows Jesus as Rabbi," Bible Scholars, https://www.biblescholars.org/2013/05/study-shows-jesus-as -rabbi.html.
2. Mark A. Noll, *The Scandal of the Evangelical Mind* (Grand Rapids, MI: Eerdmans, 1994), 3.
3. Augustine, *The Confessions*, Augustinian Heritage Institute translation, (Hyde Park, NY: New City Press, 1997), Book 7, Section 10, 166–167.
4. Richard Bevan, "The Lost Years of Jesus: The Mystery of Christ's Missing 18 Years," Sky History, https://www.history.co.uk/articles/the-lost-years -of-jesus-what-was-he-doing-in-those-missing-18-years.
5. "10 Spiritual Disciplines to Strengthen Your Faith," Cru, accessed November 15, 2023, https://www.cru.org/us/en/train-and-grow/spiritual -growth/spiritual-disciplines-strengthen-faith.html.

CHAPTER 3: BUILD

1. Sabine R. Huebner, *Papyri and the Social World of the New Testament* (Cambridge: Cambridge University Press, 2019), 66.
2. Sean McDowell, "What Was It like for Jesus to Be a Carpenter?", SeanMcDowell.org, January 11, 2022, https://seanmcdowell.org/blog /what-it-was-like-for-jesus-to-be-a-carpenter.

CHAPTER 4: BELONG

1. Matt Perman, "What Is the Doctrine of the Trinity?" Desiring God, January 23, 2006, https://www.desiringgod.org/articles/what-is -the-doctrine-of-the-trinity.
2. In the third century, the theological heresy of modalism arose. This heresy embraced the belief that God is just one God and Father, Son, and Holy Spirit are really just different expressions of the one God.

CHAPTER 7: PURIFY

1. Ted Olsen, "The Life & Times of Jesus of Nazareth: Did You Know?" *Christianity Today*, https://www.christianitytoday.com/history/issues /issue-59/life-times-of-jesus-of-nazareth-did-you-know.html.

CHAPTER 8: LOVE

1. Rosaria Champagne, "Promise Keepers' Message Is a Threat to Democracy," *The Post-Standard* (Syracuse, NY), April 15, 1997, 9.

CHAPTER 9: FOLLOW

1. Ann Spangler and Lois Tverberg, *Sitting at the Feet of Rabbi Jesus: How the Jewishness of Jesus Can Transform Your Faith* (Grand Rapids, MI: Zondervan, 2009), 51.

2. You can read more about my story in my memoir, *Unlikely Fighter: The Story of How a Fatherless Street Kid Overcame Violence, Chaos, and Confusion to Become a Radical Christ Follower* (Carol Stream, IL: Tyndale, 2021).

CHAPTER 10: PRAY

1. You can read more of Crystal Miller's story in her books *Marked for Life*, *A Kids Book about School Shootings*, and *A Kids Book about School Shootings for Survivors*.

CHAPTER 12: PROCLAIM

1. GOSPEL acrostic copyright © Dare 2 Share and used by permission.

2. Charles Haddon Spurgeon, "Preaching for the Poor," *New Park Street Pulpit*, vol. 3, The Spurgeon Center, January 25, 1857, https://www .spurgeon.org/resource-library/sermons/preaching-for-the-poor/#flipbook/.

3. Walter W. Oetting, *The Church of the Catacombs: An Introduction to the Surging Life of the Early Church from the Apostles to A.D. 250 Based on Firsthand Accounts* (St. Louis: Concordia, 1964), 24.

CHAPTER 15: ABIDE

1. Francis A. Schaeffer, *True Spirituality* (Carol Stream, IL: Tyndale House, 1971 (2012 edition)), 71.

2. Major W. Ian Thomas, "Torchbearers Was Born out of Brokenness," Torchbearers International, accessed November 29, 2023, https://torchbearers.org/who-we-are/history.

CHAPTER 16: WRESTLE

1. Philip Yancey, "Praying All the Way to the Bank," *Philip Yancey* (blog), May 18, 2020, https://philipyancey.com/praying-all-the-way-to-the-bank.

CHAPTER 17: SUFFER

1. E. M. Hall (lyrics) and J. T. Grape (composer), "Jesus Paid It All" originally published under the title "Fullness in Christ," *Sabbath Carols*, ed. Theodore E. Perkins (New York: Brown & Perkins, 1868), 93.

CHAPTER 18: FORGIVE

1. Corrie ten Boom with Elizabeth and John Sherrill, *The Hiding Place* (Grand Rapids, MI: Chosen Books, 2006), 247–248.

About the Author

GREG STIER is an evangelist, author, church planter, and prophetic voice to the global church. He is the founder and visionary of Dare 2 Share—a ministry that has mobilized millions of teenagers and adults to share the gospel with clarity and confidence. Greg is the author of more than twenty books, including his memoir, *Unlikely Fighter: The Story of How a Fatherless Street Kid Overcame Violence, Chaos, and Confusion to Become a Radical Christ Follower.* He has been interviewed by Focus on the Family, CBN, CNN, and Fox News about his passion, the power of the gospel, and the potential of teenagers. He won't stop until every teen everywhere hears the gospel from a friend. Greg lives in Denver with his wife of thirty-three years, Debbie, and has two adult children, Jeremy and Kailey.

GREG
STIER

SPEAKING REQUESTS
gregstier.org/speaking

BLOG
gregstier.org

For more resources
to help you live a
revolutionary life, visit
gregstier.org/radicallikejesus.

FOLLOW